THE BEST OF PRIVATE EYE
1994

ALSO AVAILABLE FROM PRIVATE EYE • CORGI

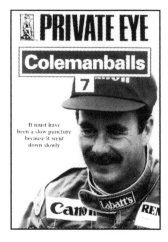

**The 3rd & last
SECRET DIARY OF
JOHN MAJOR**
This is the third collection of John Major's
celebrated Secret Diary and it might be
prudent to allow that it could in some
measure be the not unfinal one.
£4.99

RUN FOR COVER
A Collection of the Best Eye Covers
from the last fve years
£5.99

COLEMANBALLS 7
Even more unbelievable
utterances from Private Eye's
most amazing column
£3.99

Published in Great Britain by Private Eye Productions Ltd
6 Carlisle Street, London W1V 5RG
in association with Corgi Books

©1994 Pressdram Ltd
ISBN 0 552 14277 8
Designed by Bridget Tisdall
Printed in England by Ebenezer Baylis & Son Ltd, Worcester

Corgi Books are published by Transworld Publishers Ltd 61–63 Uxbridge Road, Ealing, London W5 5SA
in Australia by Transworld Publishers (Australia) Pty, Ltd 15–23 Helles Avenue, Moorebank, NSW 2170
and in New Zealand by Transworld Publishers (N.Z.) Ltd 3 William Pickering Drive, Albany, Auckland.

2 4 6 8 10 9 7 5 3 1

ABSOLUTELY LIBELLOUS

Edited by Ian Hislop

PRIVATE EYE • CORGI

UPFRONTERS

☺ It must be computer dating! **Sharon Stone's** definitely sweet on **Alan Sugar!** He won't need any Hot-spurring on with this Tottynam either!

☺ Joely good show! Miss **Richardson** is one maiden who has been bowled over by dishy **David Gower!** She may have been Lady Chatterley but he's not at Lords! Are they going out or staying in!

☺ Who's this with stars in his eyes? It's TV's **Patrick Moore** looking at the heavenly body of **Amanda de Cadenet!** Is that a telescope in your pocket Patrick or are you just pleased to see her?

☺ You Who!! It's **Roger Daltrey** of course and she's a **Britt** of alright too! They're talking 'bout his generation, I expect! Still, there will always be an **Eckland**!

☺ **Caine** and a Belle! **Raquel Welch** is certainly keeping herself under wraps! Not many people know that! What a Welch rare bit!

☺ Lord Linley's fiancé is looking calm and **Serena!** Though her escort **Sir Peregrine** is looking somewhat the **Worsthorne** for wear!! Don't build up your **Stan-hopes** Perry! This girl's already viscounted for!

(That's enough piss poor captions to PR photos by clapped out hacks, Ed.)

The Rising Sunday Telegraph

Friday, 18 June, 1993   2bn Yen

Prince and Princess Vow Undying Hatred

by Our Man in London **Harry Kiri**

BEHIND locked doors and hidden from the eyes of the world, the British Prince Chazza Luni and the Princess Fookee-Squidgee yesterday acted out the age-old rite of Separation by Mutual Consent, by which British couples pledge their lasting dislike of each other, and agree to remain apart except for what is known as *access*.

This almost mystical practice traditionally involves the father taking his children to the famous Zoological Gardens in London on alternate Sunday afternoons, while his wife engages in the Tantric Yoga discipline known as *legova*.

Prince of Killing Wales

Yesterday's awesome ceremony, which millions of disloyal subjects did not see, centres on the unloving

couple being shut away with a ceremonial attendant, known as Lord Goodmanzee, to agree the traditional "Terms of Settlement".

But, before that, many ritual preliminaries have to be enacted, in the seclusion of the marital home. First, the couple must exchange certain ritual cries. The Princess shouts "Yushit" and the Prince replies "Yukau".

The Princess then raises the sacred rolling pin and places it on the Prince's head with a sharp downward movement, to symbolise her innermost feelings of distaste for her husband.

He then makes answer by rais-

ing the Holy Book of Morton, containing sacred texts inspired by the Princess's own words, and throwing it at her head to symbolise his desire to do her a very serious injury.

At this point, Lord Goodmanzee is helped back into the room to present them with his bill, and the couple live unhappily ever after.

A Haiku for the Royal Separation
by the Poet Laureate Ted Hoo Hee

Old Whaley in sea.
Bang.
Harpoon in blubber.
Blood froths.
Whaley washed up (on beach).
(Will this do? T.H.)
(No, too many syllables, Ed.)

Trans. by Sir Arthur Whaley

LADY THATCHERSLEY'S LOVER

by Ken Russell Grant

Adapted from an original story by D.H. Laurens van der Post

(Music — Bragg Fair by Delius Smith — plays on soundtrack. Shot of vintage car drawing up outside castle. Dashing young former Defence Procurement Minister jumps out and runs up steps)

Alan Clark *(for it is he):* Hullo, darling, sorry I'm late again. I was held up at the office trying to sell a Supergun to Johnny Wog.

Mrs Clark *(for it is she):* That's a ridiculous excuse, you little shit. *(Throws axe at his head)* I know where you've been. You've been with that woman again.

(Cut to Great Hall at Chequers. Sir Denis Thatchersley sitting with rug over knees, clutching large whisky glass, holding forth to his old clubland crony Lord Deedes)

Sir Clifford: So there I was, Bill, at the thirteenth, with these three Hun businessmen coming up behind me…

Deedes: Ha, ha, ha. I'll have another one.

Lady Thatchersley: I'm so bored.

Audience: So are we.

Ken Russell: I'd better put some sex in, or the BBC won't buy it.

Lady Thatchersley: I'm going for a walk in the woods. I may be some time.

(Cut to shot of Lady Thatchersley running naked in slow motion through wood. Elgar plays loudly. Small faun-like figure seen dancing in sunlit glade in Chelsea strip)

David Mellors *(for it is he):* Where's tha runnin' to, lady? I'd like to sook thy toes. 'appen I would.

Clark *(entering through trees):* I say, piss off, you little grammar school oik. She's mine, I tell you, all mine.

(Mellors runs off to write piece about latest opera CDs for Grauniad)

Clark *(going up to Lady Thatchersley and eyeing her adoringly from behind):* What a gorgeous creature you are, to be sure! You've got spiffy ankles. A fabulous pair of Bristols. And, oh heaven!, your handbag drives a man wild, d'you hear me?

(Music changes to Vaughan

Williams's 'The Clark Ascending') Would you like to see my Supergun?

Thatchersley: Oh, you are naughty. But I love you.

(Wagner swells to climax)

"I must speak seriously to Mellors"

THAT HISTORIC SHOCKING LAMONT BOMBSHELL SPEECH IN FULL

❝❝Members of the House. I have no intention in this personal statement of complaining about the fact that I was quite wrongly sacked by the Government. My only concern is to urge the need for an independent central bank, which I was working towards when I was so unjustifiably removed from office by a weak, vacillating, short-sighted Government in glasses. A Government which, I must tell the House, does not know where he is going. And who is totally under the spell of a certain Party manager, whom I shall not name but whose name begins with 'F'. All politicians want nowadays is 36 hours of cheap publicity. But not me. I want it for a lot longer. In my opinion, Mr John Government is a total bastard *(whinges on in similar vein for several hours).***❞❞**

"Hi — can I read you some of my poems?"

LIVES OF THE SAINTS NO.94

St Diana of Bulimia

Born into a rich, aristocratic family in 1961, Diana grew up in an entirely conventional way. Her parents divorced, she married the future King of England and might easily have continued to live a comfortable, obscure life as a queen and mother for the rest of her days. Then in 1992 came the dramatic series of visions which were to transform her life. She began to hear voices in the night, calling her from afar. "That you, Squidgy, has he gone out? You're wonderful, you're just divine." True to her new calling, Diana realised that she must renounce her husband and follow her vocation — making speeches about the importance of marriage and the family.

Wherever she went crowds would gather, shouting: "This way, Di, give us a smile, isn't she lovely, poor thing?" She became the most loved person in the world, and in 1993 she was finally canonised by a solemn conclave of the Editors of *Hello!* magazine.

Many miracles were performed in her name, such as the making of Andrew Morton into a wealthy man, and ridding England of its monarchy.

© Lady Antonia Holden

Lines on the Historic Opening of a McDonalds Restaurant in Hampstead

by William "Big"- MacGonagall

'Twas on June 7th in the year nineteen hundred and ninety-three,
That the folk of Hampstead made gastronomic history.
For it was on that day that McDonalds opened their burger bar,
And American tourists came to queue there from both near and
from far.

But for many a long year the opening had been delayed
Due to the Hampstead intellectuals and the fuss they made.
"We do not want our high street filled with rabble,"
Argued the likes of Tom Conti, Michael Foot and
Ms Margaret Drabble.

And there were many others who presented something of a snag,
Including the host of the South Bank Show, Mr Melvyn Bragg.
They petitioned mightily in the courts, did this prestigious
literary pack
In the hope of stopping Ronald McDonald and his famous
Big Mac.

But sadly after 12 years their case began to flounder
As other residents decided they would quite like a
quarter-pounder.
All the aesthetic arguments of the anti-McDonald lobby
Only made the judge think that they were being a wee bit snobby.

So it was decided at last that not far from the historic Heath,
McDonalds could sell beverages that are known to rot the teeth.
To accompany of course their burgers, each one carefully
polystyrene-boxed,
Where once antiquarian booksellers had sold First Editions
(slightly foxed).

And so it came to pass in the leafy Hampstead venue
McDonalds proudly displayed their full all day and
breakfast menu.
And the literati had bitterly to watch the 17-year-olds stuffing
Their faces with the famous world-renowned Egg McMuffin.

© William Rees MacGonagall

Young Telegraph Guide To Those Amazing Dinosaurs!

As seen everywhere else

Here they are:

■ **Tyrrificbaurus:** *Most frighteningly dull of all the Dinobaurs.*

■ **Megabaurus Rigid:** *Slow, heavy, but still terrifyingly uninteresting.*

■ **Supersnaurus:** *Gigantic dinobaur that rendered victims helpless by putting them to sleep.*

■ **Steggeringlybaurus:** *Much as its name suggests.*

■ **Pterriblydull:** *Flew through the air, but was no more interesting for it.*

■ **Diplodocumentary:** *Extraordinarily boring programme on all channels about the making of Jurassic Park.*

(That's enough Dinobaurs. Ed.)

"C.R. will see you now"

THE BETJEMAN LETTERS

In 1932 the young John Betjeman fell madly in love with Lady Camilla Sibbling-Rivalry, the sister of his Oxford friend Lord Brian de Walden. He called her by the affectionate name "Yellow Pages" and wrote her passionate letters all that summer.
June 14th 1932

Dear Snoopy,
It was wizard to see you at Archie's bash at Droppings. I'm so sorry Patrick crashed the car in the flower bed and was so beastly to Dumpling. I suppose he'll get over it. Won't you come with us to Casteloony next month, I want to show you the church at Bally High which has a wonderful reredos by Sir Gavin Stamp?

Love and kisses,
Your Bunty xxx

NOTE:
"Archie" was Lord Randolph Sowerbutt, the brother-in-law of Betjeman's Marlborough friend, Harry Doggers, known to his friends as extremely boring.

(Continued all week)

Betjeman (right) and Lord Anglepoyse at Oxford

HESELTINE GETS REPRIEVE

by Our Industrial Staff **Alan Coronary**

IN A dramatic U-turn yesterday, Death (the President of the Board of Grim Reaping) gave Heseltine a last chance after threatening to close him down for good.

The disputed Heseltine had been described by critics as "unproductive" and "without a long-term future" and Death had put him on the infamous "Hit List".

But yesterday, after considering alternative options (including the comparative uselessness of the rest of the Cabinet), Dezza, as he is affectionately known, decided there was no option but to keep Heseltine going.

"This is a temporary measure," he warned, "and I will be reviewing the situation periodically."

Biggles Flies A Desk
by Capt. W.E. JohnMajors

"**B**AD news, Ginger," said Squadron Leader "Biggles" Bigglesworth as he wrestled with the controls of the Canon NK473D photocopier. "I'm afraid we've lost the whole bally squadron."

"Cripes!" said Ginger as he reloaded the A4 paper into the Fax machine.

"Yes, I'm afraid we're all grounded. The whole RAF. Jerry came in at 4 o'clock."

"What Jerry from the Ministry of Defence?"

"Yes. We didn't see him coming. He started firing immediately. We tried to get him off our backs by telling him to sack everyone in the Navy instead but it was too late."

Ginger nervously checked his instruments. Pencil sharpener, rubber band, Post-it note dispenser. All AOK. Biggles continued, his upper lip stiffening visibly: "We put up a good fight but we've had to ditch all the crates and most of the lads aren't coming back."

"We're no match for those dashed P45s are we, Sir?"

"Apparently not, Ginger. Some of the chaps baled out into Civvy Street in time but the rest just crashed onto the old dole."

There was a long pause and Ginger looked shaken as he made a slow 180 degree turn round the coffee machine.

"Buck up, Ginge!" Biggles reassured his old chum. "At least we can still fly this old kite."

"What is it, sir? Tornado? Harrier? Phantom?"

"No, it's a kite. I bought it at Hamley's"

"Tally ho, Sir!"

Lines Written On The Decision Of The BBC Not To Continue The That's Life Programme After 25 Historic Years

by William Rees-McGonegall

'Twas in the year Nineteen Hundred and Ninety Three
That a momentous decision was taken by the BBC.
To terminate the celebrated programme called That's Life
Which at one time was watched by millions, e.g. Mr Average
                              Briton and his wife.

No longer could the nation look forward to weekends
To tune into Miss Rantzen and her young male friends.
No longer would they see her gleaming teeth
Or the black-stocking-ed legs that she displayed beneath.

Over the years she had become the conscience of the nation
As her exposés forced small businessmen into liquidation.
Many a time-share seller rued the day
When Esther and her film crew came down their way.

Also the Gas Board was in no position to rejoice
When its spokesmen were quoted in a silly voice.
Esther presided over it all like a glamorous granny
Acting as TV's leading Super-Nanny.

In her wake came her little band of Young Turks
Thought by many to be no more than a bunch of emasculated
                              jerks.
(Surely "brilliant investigative journalists exposing the waterworks?")
One thinks of such names as Chris Searle and Doc Cox
And there were many such others who owed to her their career
                              on the box.

But the programme of course had its lighter side
To balance the sad stories of punters who'd been taken for a ride.
Many a dog was persuaded to stand up and sing
And budgies were seen to perform acrobatic manoeuvres on
                              their swing.

Indeed an episode was considered a failure
That did not show a carrot which looked like male genitalia.
Older viewers will recall Mr. Fletcher sitting in his special chair
As Esther said to him "Cyril have you got a cutting for us there?"

"Yes Esther" the aged entertainer would reply
"It concerns the opening of a new public toilet in Rye".
Such merry jests were greeted by the studio audience with
                              such laughter
That Esther must have thought her show would go on for
                              ever after.

In the streets of West London she became a famous figure
Wandering about always trying to raise a snigger.
"What does this remind you of, madam?" she would cry
Waving a large pink sausage in an old lady's eye.

And if they didn't say something silly
She'd move on until someone cried "It's a willy".
But eventually after many a long year the ratings began to fall
Until there was no one left watching That's Life at all.

So in desperation they moved it to Saturday night
But viewers preferred to go down the pub to get tight.
So finally it was left to Mr Yentob, Head of BBC1
To tell Esther the dread news that her long day was done.

And so she was tossed onto the scrapheap of history
And what she will do next remains at the time of writing a
mystery.

© William Rees-McGonagall 1993

"Did you pack your trunk yourself, Ms Elephant"

FLOOD CHAOS LATEST

THIS morning bemused residents are still counting the cost of the worst floods in living memory after they hit the House of Lords.

It happened during a debate on the Maastricht Bill and there was little or no warning. The Missithatchi suddenly burst her banks and poured out millions of gallons of muddy water all over the Upper House.

Said one gnarled old survivor: "It was terrible. One minute I was asleep, the next I was engulfed in this overpowering torrent. I tell you, never underestimate the power of the ol' Missithatchi. Nowadays she may look pretty slow-moving but deep down she's just waiting to swallow us all up, yes, sirree."

DINOSAUR TERROR STALKS FLEET STREET

by Our Fossil Correspondent
Charlotte Brontosaurus

THOUSANDS fled in terror yesterday as hundreds of prehistoric cliches ran amok across the broadsheets, causing panic and boredom to sweep the land.

A swarm of metaphors not seen in such numbers since the last dinosaur movie (*Raquel Whatsername in 2,000,000 Years BC —*

Ed.) spread uncontrollably across London, mutating into terrifyingly unfunny jokes such as 'The Maastrichtodon' (*Grauniad*) and 'Thatcherosaurus Rex' (*Observer*). Inspector "Knacker of the Yard" Knacker said: "We had the situation under control, with all the metaphorsauruses safely confined within the minds of a few ageing hacks, then some irresponsible lout released an overhyped film (*shurely 'all the dinosaurs'? Ed*).

— PILBROW —

CROP CIRCLE STORIES BEGIN TO REAPPEAR

by Our Not-On-Holiday Staff **Mike Standin** and **Sandra Work-Experience**

AMAZING crop circle stories have been spotted all over Britain's newspapers this week.

For the first time since last summer an outbreak of these extraordinary phenomena has again baffled readers looking for news.

Said one spotter: "I've no idea why they keep coming back year after year. But they are definitely back. On Tuesday I saw seven, with a beautiful one in the *Telegraph*. It was an extraordinary shape, going down the first column and then round and round an advertisement for memory loss."

Once again experts have offered various explanations for the recurrence of these summer paranormal manifestations. They suggest they are caused by:

● **Electrical impulses** swirling on the geodesic axis of the globe.

● **Extraterrestrial life forms giving a coded message via the pages of the *Independent*.**

● **Desperate journalists filling in all the acres of space whilst the entire Features staff is on holiday in Tuscany.**

One thing is certain. No one knows where they will appear next, but a pretty good guess is to look between the stories about Diana going shopping and the ones about her not going shopping.

ET has gone home.

ON OTHER PAGES ● *Article held over since April p 3* ● *Piece that wouldn't normally get in p 4* ● *Simon Heffer on something or other p 6* ● *Big photos pp 5, 7, 9, 10* ● *Thin stuff pp 11, 12, 13, 15, 17, 18*

Places to go: things to do – with kids in mind

● Open Day at **Neasden Reservoir.**
A fascinating excursion for all the family to one of north London's newest reservoirs (1978). Includes visit to the computerised Control Room, Filter Complex and Perimeter Walk. Aug. 27th. Admission £3. Concessions £2. (Neasden Tube or 147B bus)

● **The Norris Moth Museum, Bath.**
An excellent small museum which boasts over 3,000 species of moth from Europe and North America. There are audio-visual displays and a hands-on Moth Simulator which older youngsters will love. Informative Personal Tour by curator Christopher Norris, nephew of the founder Randolph Norris. Aug 3rd-Oct 27. Admission free — Donations welcome. (A94, Junction 10)

● **The Lymeswold Working Cheese Museum, Buddleigh Salterton.**
Britain's only fully functional cheese-producing learning centre, with an entire 18th-century Cheesery recreated in an old windmill. The staff wear exciting period costumes and youngsters take home a free piece of cheese. Family admission £12. (M7, Northwich Turn-Off)

● **The Chuter-Ede Walk, Streatham.**
An urban walk in the footsteps of famous 'Fifties Labour Cabinet Minister James Chuter-Ede through his old constituency. 1½ hours with guide includes his house in Glenolden Road, the public library he opened in 1958, and the housing development named after him (subsequently renamed The Bernie Grant Estate). 2.30pm every 2nd Wednesday, August through to November. Admission £28.50. No concessions. (Brixton Tube or 159 bus)

● **The Crack Factory, Stoke Newington.**
All-night trip to the biggest crack/cocaine centre in Europe. Meet Mr Death and go for a joyride in a stolen Ford Cosworth. *(Shouldn't this be the Cricklewood Ceramics Centre, where you can watch potters at their wheel making a variety of household crockery and where kids can take home a Personalised Horoscope Mug? Ed.)*

RESEARCH: Deborah Drear, Kevin Beard, Felicity Grunge, Roger Alton, Polly Pilkin and Iain McDullie.

CORRECTION
The Peruvian Alta Rica Band, who we listed in last week's guide as performing outdoors at the Yeovil Leisure Centre on 27th July, were in fact playing at the One World Children's Fair in Skegness.

The Glamis Herald

Macbeth defends wife – 'Saintly, selfless public servant' says former Thane

by HENRY THE PORTER

THE controversial new king of Scotland, King Macbeth, today spoke out in defence of his wife, Lady Hillary Macbeth, whom many critics have called "the power behind the throne".

Cawdor What A Scorcher

At an emotional press conference in the dungeon of the Castle, the king told scribes of his deep distress over the recent "Duncangate" allegations.

● It is rumoured that the unexpected death of King Duncan, a close member of the Macbeth circle, may well have had something to do with the Macbeths and Lady Macbeth in particular.

● It is further claimed that the suicide of long-term Macbeth associate, Banquo, may also have had a political motive.

But the king firmly rebutted any such reports, saying: "My wife has the finest moral compass of anyone I know." He also said that the allegations had left Lady Macbeth very distressed and that she had had to call in medical help following attacks of sleepwalking.

Banker's Ghost

There were also unconfirmed reports that the King himself had been subject to hallucinations and that a recent reception at the castle had to called off suddenly after the king was "taken ill".

Suggestions that the king may have "seen ghosts" after indulging in marijuana were dismissed by an official spokesman.

Weather Forecast for Tomorrow and Tomorrow and Tomorrow

With IAN MACBETHKILL

A LARGE area of trees is now on the move in the Birnam area which is expected to reach Dunsinane by tomorrow midday.

Cooking Tips

with THE WEIRD SISTERS

TAKE ONE Eye of Newt, one Toe of Frog, one Wool of Bat and one Tongue of Dog. Bring to the boil and put in the microwave in a non-metallic receptacle. *(Shurely shome mishtake?)*

On Other Pages

St Cakes

Howard Term starts today. There are 4,516 video nasties in the School Shop. H.J.Q. Childs-Play III (Winner's) is Head of Porn. R.R.B. Brain-Dead (Murdoch's) is Senior Sky Warden and Keeper of the Dish. The Rev B. Mephistoles-Beelzebub (OC) will conduct Satanic Rituals in Witch's Field on 21st June (Walhennessynacht). There will be a performance of *Chainsaw Massacre* by the St Cakes Dramatic Society in the Sunday Sport Hall on 8th July. Tickets from the Bursar, Derek Beackon, Wapping, Tower Hamlets Road, BNP 666. Snuffings will be on 16 July.

Poetry Corner

In Memoriam Kurt Cobain, Lead Singer Of The Popular Grunge Singing Group Nirvana

So. Farewell then
Kurt Cobain.

You shot yourself
Because you were
Depressed.

I once listened
To one of your
Records.

So I know
How you
Must have felt.

E.J. Thribb (17½)

"Problem, Midas?"

Notes & Queries

QUESTION: Who invented chips?

☐ YOUR correspondent from Yorkshire, J.R. Hattersley, is only partially correct in claiming that it was Isaac Braithwaite of Ilkley who first concocted what we now recognise as chips in 1796. Braithwaite, a wealthy potato merchant, had travelled extensively through Europe and whilst in northern France had stayed overnight at a small Benedictine monastery in Caen. He recorded in his diary on 7 November 1794:

"Last night we dined on an extraordinary dish which the Breton monks refer to as 'les chips'. They are made by throwing slivers of finger-length potato into a pan of sizzling pork fat. They are then eaten hot and served folded in a copy of the previous day's news journal, in this case *Le Soleil* of 6th November."

Clearly Braithwaite took the formula home to Yorkshire where two years later he introduced it, as Hattersley noted, in lieu of wages to his itinerant Irish work force. — *Mr P.B.R. Golden-Wonder, Finchley.*

QUESTION: Is it true, as was recently suggested, that George Washington was Jewish?

☐ THERE is some circumstantial evidence to support this claim, made in the recently published book *So Now I'm Telling Lies?* by Professor Lionel Blueberry of Princeton University. Blueberry's thesis relies on a little-known incident when Washington first took office as President. The menu for his inauguration lunch, which was lavish even by the standard of the times, included a large hamburger known as a "Yankee Doodle Double". However it was noted by a guest, the Marquis de Spencer, that the new President had eaten everything except the hamburger, which was of course forbidden to Orthodox Jews like Washington because it contained ham. — *Rabbi Julia Hamburger, London.*

QUESTION: Who was the first person to wear a moustache?

☐ EVERYONE who has written on this subject to date is wrong. Largely because they are incapable of viewing the question from outside the Eurocentric bias. 1,000 years before Prince Häagen-Dazs of Bohemia sported a hairy upper lip (Mr J. Oxleas, 7 March 1992) and 500 years before Wogan the Jute did the same (B.M. Twyford's contribution on 28 January 1991), the Ottoman Emperor Achmed ben Mushtaq III, decreed that no

"You know your trouble – you listen too much"

male over the age of 16 could shave his facial hair above the lip "upon pain of death". Instituted as a memorial to his brother Mohammed Mushtaq, who had died in a shaving accident during the Third Mesopotamian War, the fashion for an unshaved upper lip quickly spread through the ancient world and became known as "the Mushtaq" or "Moustache". (See other eponyms such as Wellington, Sandwich, Trouser-Press.) — *Günther Gillette, Institute of Trichological Research, Zurich.*

NEXT WEEK: Answers please for the following: Where are we? Do the Swiss Army use their knives? Do bananas cause male-pattern baldness? Do crabs see colours? What's Donald Trelford up to nowadays?

CLINTON: OFFICIAL NEW PORTRAIT

Behind every successful woman there's an unsuccessful man

EDINBURGH HIGHLIGHTS

What to see and where to see it at the biggest festival in Edinburgh this year

COMEDY

Billy Tosser

Tosser is an explosive mixture of Jack Dee, Eddie Izzard, Sean Hughes and Elton John *(shurely 'Ben Elton'? Ed).* His new one-man show is sharp, rude and already sold out so you can't go. Bad luck. You'll probably get in to see Jimmy Jerk who, to be honest, is much the same. Look out for his hard-hitting lager advert on the telly. The Golden Marquee. Midnight, most nights.

DANCE

Hoppy Rap Rocker and the Kicking Hotshots

Exuberant modern dance from the Seattle Ballet combining elements of tap, jive and classical ballet set to music from Bernstein to James Last. Be warned that there are scenes of explicit tedium *(shurely 'nudity'? Ed)* throughout the show. The Grand House. All November.

FILM

The Concrete Fish

Moving autobiographical story of a remembered childhood in a small Swedish village in the 1950s. A lovingly shot masterpiece by Swedish filmmaker Jørn Nonstøp. Winner of the Guernsey Palm d'Or (Best Autobiographical Swedish Film Set In Small Village In The 1950s). The Cameo. 1-3 September.

DRAMA

Awa' Ye English Bastards

Tautly written trilogy of new plays by young Scottish playwright Donald McWhinge, winner of the Hebridean Silver Medal For First Trilogies About How Awful The English Are, 1993. Assembly Hall, 19-27 August. 10 hours. No concessions to being interesting *(shurely 'to students'? Ed).*

ART

The Mirror

An exhibition of photographs by Canadian artist Kodak Brownie showing members of the public looking at last year's exhibition of photographs by Kodak Brownie showing scenes of rural Saskatchewan under snow. Brilliantly dull *(shurely 'composed'? And anyway that's enough Edinburgh. Ed).* The Scottish Academy 12-13 January.

WHO SAYS IT ISN'T WORKING?

IN recent weeks there have been many claims that the Government's policy of Care in the Community isn't working. But here is the proof that releasing the mentally impaired back into the community can bring happiness to everyone involved. Mrs B. is totally mad — yet here she is harmlessly enjoying a seaside holiday, just like anyone else. She is surrounded by her family and friends just as if she was "normal".

CARE IN THE COMMUNITY
Better Out Than In!

Issued by the Department of Health and Propaganda

NEVERLAND RAIDED SHOCK

by Our Showbiz Staff

Lunchtime A'Buse

Mr Pan

THE WORLD of entertainment was rocked to its foundations yesterday as police raided the hideaway home of one of the world's most famous children's entertainers.

Allegations have recently emerged about Peter Pan and his alleged relationship with various "lost boys" whom Mr Pan is said to have befriended and entertained at his fantasy retreat (located near the second star on the left).

Taking the Michael

Police Commissioner Captain Hook said: "This time I've got Pan. He's finished." His assistant Police Sergeant Smee said: "One of the lost boys' mothers has given us detailed evidence of how Pan slept with her son near Hangman's Tree on a number of occasions and even called him Darling."

Mrs Darling is attempting to bring serious charges against Mr Pan but the entertainer's associates insist that the stories are all make-believe and that the whole affair is part of a blackmail attempt.

Showbiz friends are also sticking by him, and Elizabeth Tinkerbell has flown in especially in order to comfort the beleaguered star in his hour of need.

Peter "Wacko" Pan has long been a mystery to commentators – the little boy who never grew up, living out a childish dream entirely removed from reality. Says one leading psychologist: "Peter is a very disturbed boy. He has become detached from his own shadow. It does not surprise me that he seeks the company of children like John Darling, Michael Darling and Macaulay Caulkin." (*Surely 'Wendy Darling'? — Ed.*)

Loonwalk

Peter Pan last night cancelled an appearance in the sky. "He's sick," said a close associate. "He's really sick," added Captain Hook with an evil cackle as he sealed off Neverland for good and dredged the Mermaid Lagoon for further evidence.

Pan himself has refused to answer the allegations directly, saying only that: "All I ever wanted to do was abuse children." (*Shurely 'amuse'? — Ed.*)

Peter Pan is still 11.

St Cakes heads 'A' Level league table

The independent school of St Cakes in Eccles has once again topped the 'A' Level failure league with only two 'A' Level passes being achieved. J.R. Hartley (Pages) gained a "D" grade in Media Studies and R.R.R. Bodyform (Rayner's) scored an "E" grade in Creative Counselling.

That List In Full:

1. The Yusuf Islam Ismalia Institute For Boys, Neasden. 100% of Pupils gained a Distinction in 'A' Level Islamic History (Special Paper: "Why Rushdie Must Die").

2. The Yusuf Islam Ismalia Institute For Girls, Neasden. 100% of pupils gained a Distinction in 'A' Level Islamic Domestic Science (Special Paper: "Why Rushdie Must Die").

3. Blessed Arnold Goodman's, Finchley. 120% of pupils gained Passes in Libel Studies *(shurely 'Liberal Studies'? Ed)*.

4. The Rees-Mogg School, Taunton. 100% of pupils failed on 'A' Level British Constitution.

(That's enough League Table, EdMaster.)

I must get a bigger bed

FLEET STREET'S MAD COW!?!

GLENDA SLAGG

THE GAL WITH THE SIX YEAR OLD BEEF!

CALL me old-fashioned, but I thought people were assoomed innocent till they've been proven guilty?!! Isn't that right, Mr Pressman?!! So why for Gawd's sake is Wacko Jacko tried and hung by the Meejah before he even knows what he's accused of!?! Frankly it makes me ashamed to be a journalist!?!?!

WACKO Jacko!? What a perv?!! A-creepin' and a-sleepin' with little lads scarcely out of short pants!?!

URGHHH! He says "I'm Bad"!? Well, now we know!? Crawl back into the sewer Mr Molester and keep your filthy hands off the fans!?! Geddit!?!

MICHAEL Jackson!?! Doesn't he make yer flesh crawl?!? *(You've done this one, Ed.)*

WACKO Jacko!? *(Look, I told you. Do someone else. Ed.)*

DIDJA read about the wife-swappin' policemen who traded in their Missis for the ladies next door?!?!! What a couple of bent coppers!?! No wonder they called them PC69!?! *(Geddit?!)* How sickening!?! It's almost as sickenin' as that Michael Jackson, what a bender!?! *(You're fired, Ed.)*

HERE they are, Glenda's Satellite Dishes!?!

● **NIGEL SHORT**!?! What's your first move, Big Boy!? Why don't we take a knight off together and go for some pawn?! Geddit?

● **LUCIAN FREUD**?!! Ok, so he's old and wrinkled but he lets it all hang out!?!! Mmmm!?!

● **TRISTAN GAREL-JONES**. Crazy name, crazy guy!?

Byeee!?!

MERCY FLIGHT GIVES HOPE FOR WAR VICTIM

by Our Medical Correspondent **Lunchtime O'Bosnia**

IT WAS a pitiful sight. Little John Major was lying at the bottom of the polls with little chance of survival. The experts had almost given up. And then came a miracle. Suddenly there was a chance that John's popularity could be airlifted to safety by a single flight into Sarajevo.

A nation held its breath as Operation Major got under way and the most famous victim of the lack of fighting was at last given the treatment by the newspapers that he so desperately required.

Before, his condition had been critical. The team looking after him had neither the resources nor the talent to halt his decline.

"We thought he would go under," said spin-doctor O'Donnell. "We gave him a few weeks at most. Time was running out and the polls weren't responding at all, whatever we did."

The doctor explained that although they had tried keeping him quiet and not letting him do anything, the only thing that would save him was a massive injection of good publicity. "And you just can't get that in London," said the spin-doctor. "You have to go to Bosnia."

LATE NEWS

Controversy has now broken out after a number of other casualties tried to get in on the airlift. Said an official: "It's disgraceful. The Italians and the French are trying to benefit as well. The whole exercise should only be for really desperate cases like Little John."

(Reuters)

Hurd and Major

by P. G. Wodehouse

(Bertie Major is discovered sitting at the piano, gazing at a picture of Aunt Magatha and singing "Anything you can do, I can't do". Hurd shimmers in carrying freshly ironed copy of Daily Telegraph on silver tray)

Major: I say, Hurd, that *Telegraph* looks dashed small.

Hurd: Indeed, sir. I have taken the liberty of excising all the articles unfavourable to yourself.

Major: Jolly thoughtful of you, old bean. *(Picks up remaining shreds of paper and begins to read)* I say, it says here that we're going to send an army of 8,000 chaps to this Bosnia place.

Hurd: Such would indeed appear to be the case.

Major: Jolly good show to us, that's what I say. *(Stands up and begins to practise golf shots with umbrella)* But hang on, Hurd. I didn't think we had 8,000 bally old warriors left. I thought we told Oofy Rifkind to pack them all off to civvy street because we were running a bit short of the readies.

Hurd: That is also the case, sir. Mr Rifkind is, I understand, in the process of carrying out your instructions with commendable Scottish zeal.

Major: Then I don't get it, Hurd. How do we square the old circle? I mean, how do we send 8,000 squarebashers off to jolly old Sara-what'shisname if we haven't got them?

Hurd: I took the precaution, sir, of adding a proviso to the promise to send in the aforementioned troops — namely that we should only send them when that unhappy country has been restored to a state of complete peace.

Major: Well, I say, Hurd, that doesn't sound very likely. At that rate they'll never be sent.

Hurd: Indeed, sir. As the Roman poet Terence so pithily observed, *rem acutus tetigisti.*

Major: I say, Hurd, you're a bally genius. Have you been tucking into the fish again? *(Begins to strum golf club and croon "Pack up your troubles in your old shitbag" from the musical Gummertime)*

Hurd: I always endeavour to give service, sir.

© *Fry & Laurie Productions, from an idea by P.G. Wodehouse.*

Notes & Queries

QUESTION: Who was the Man in the Iron Mask?

☐ For years it was believed that he was the half-brother of King Louis XXXV (Le Duc d'Ellington, 1641-?). But latest research links him to the even older legend of the Shroud of Turin. The theory is that the Knights Templar accompanied Joseph of Arimathea on his visit to Brittany where he founded a secret order of mystical warriors who guarded the Holy Grail in a hilltop fortress which later became the Albigensian stronghold of Nevers-sur-Dimanche, where in 1223 the Cathars made their last stand against (contd. 1294). — *H. Thompson, London N7.*

QUESTION: Who invented braces?

☐ The answer is not, as Mrs Lynne Barber claimed last week, Josiah Laurie of the old Jermyn Street tailoring firm Fry and Laurie. The first braces were actually made of wood and were introduced in the mid-4th century as standard wear for Roman legionnaires, to hold up the heavily armoured under-breeches (or "pantini"). These were known as *braccae*, literally "little trees", and a perfectly preserved example, excavated at the Roman villa of Fishwick, Derbyshire, can be seen in the Buxton Folk Museum. — *C. Hawtree, Brighton.*

QUESTION: What is the world's smallest fish?

☐ Sir D. Attenbore writes: When I was filming in Java in 1984 for my series *Earthwatch '84*, we were lucky to catch a glimpse of the Two-Finned Golden Bonsai Dwarf Fish, which is only 0.0001mm long and cannot be seen by the naked eye. Traditionally regarded as a powerful aphrodisiac by the native Attallah islanders, the dwarf fish is unhappily now extinct, as it requires 6 million of them to cover a small plate. Probably the smallest extant fish is the Brazilian Guppy, now in gaol on fraud charges *(see Spectator passim)*.

NEXT WEEK: Answers please for the following: Is it true that the Chinese invented tube trains in the 8th century? Can bees swim? Why do we "wave" goodbye? Why does anyone employ David Mellor?

PETER McLie

The World's Worst Columnist

Isn't it one of the most amazing things in life when you get to the railway station and find there is no shop selling ties?

Here's my idea for Sir Peter Parker.

Why not open a shop on every station selling only ties?

And I've even thought of a name for it. Sock Shop.

Isn't life dandy when you're wearing a bonny new tie?

(Brilliant stuff — you are my idea of a great journalist. B. Pad-Ed.)

● **My friend Andrew Wilson went to see this new film about a monster fish from the deep.**

He tells me it is called *Jurassic Shark.*

Apparently it is very frightening and I would recommend strongly that wee bairns should not be permitted to see it.

Whatever will they think of next? A huge gorilla standing on the Empire State Building?

☐ HAVE YOU noticed those funny little green things coming out of trees? They certainly weren't there a week ago. And yet now nearly every tree I see out of the train window has these curious unexplained little growths on them. But nobody seems to want to point this out. Is it something to do with political correctness? I however shall watch these wee green beasties with interest and until told otherwise will call them 'electric kettles'. (This is wonderful. B. Pad.)

● *You don't hear much about Mrs Thatcher nowadays.*

Isn't it a shame?

I for one would love to know what she thinks of her successor.

I have an idea for the lady.

Why doesn't she write down all her thoughts and put them in a book?

It would make a grand read, wouldn't it? And it might make her a few bawbees into the bargain.

But no doubt the publishing fraternity would be too frightened that she might say something controversial.

Isn't life grand?

☐ TEA leaves are a terrible menace, are they not? It's always hard to get them out of the pot when you are doing the washing up.

I have an idea. Why not create a small perforated container filled with tea leaves which could be placed inside the pot? There would be no mess and a fine and dandy cup of tea would be the result. What's more I have a name for it — The Filofax.

TV HIGHLIGHTS

Die Hard III (BBC2)
Starring Norman Willis

Willis is meant to have retired but trouble starts when baddie John Smith tries to hijack the TUC Conference with his dreaded OMOV weapon. Willis refuses to die. No thrills. No spills. A few tears. *(7,888 minutes)*

Summer Holiday (BBC1)
Starring Cliff Richard and Una Stubbs

Everyone in Fleet Street is on their summer holiday so someone digs up a really terrible old story about Cliff and Una having an affair. There is a happy ending as the story fills up acres of space. Songs include "The Old Ones". *(b&w)*

Billy Connolly Live (ITV)

Billy confesses that at one stage he thought of becoming "funny" but instead he shaved off his beard, went to California and made lager adverts.

(That's enough TV. Ed.)

Yes! It's Televised World Chess Championship Rhyming Slang!

Checkmate	**On too late**
Channel Four	**Terrific snore**
BBC2	**Go to the loo**
Kasparov	**Turn him off**
Nigel Short	**Which channel's the sport?**
Grandmaster	**Can't they play faster?**
GXF3	**The Bill's on ITV**
Match drawn	**Huge yawn**
Players get half	**Hardly a laugh**
Queen's knight	**No end in sight**
Chess board	**I certainly am**

(That's enough slang. Ed.)

IT'S GOOD OL' SNOOP DOGGY DOGG! BY SCHLITZ

THE JERICHO WALL STREET JOURNAL

Friday 24 September 1993 BC   2 shekels (slashed to only 3)

It's Peace At Last As Philistines Sign Historic Accord With Children Of Israel

by Our Man in Gaza SAUL JOHNSON

A 1,000-year-old conflict came to an end last night when the Chairman of the Philistine Liberation Organisation, Mr Goliath, shook hands with Israeli leader Mr David.

Mr David told waiting scribes: "This is the day the stonethrowing has to stop."

Mr Goliath agreed, saying that he looked forward to a peace between the two nations that would last for three thousand years.

Camp David

The Middle East conflict, which has already filled 14 books of the Old Testament, began when the Children of Israel took over the land of the Philistines, claiming that they were "only obeying orders" from a Mr Yahweh.

Their then-leader, General Moses Dayan, 357, claimed that he had been specifically instructed to take over the "land of milk and honey" and declare the State of Israel.

The Philistines retaliated, most notably in the Seven Hundred Years War, and continued to lay claim to the West Bank, the East Bank and the Bank of Israel.

Following the new peace settlement, further deals are expected between the Children of Israel and the Hivites, Perizzites, Jebusites and Moabites.

On Other Pages

A Doctor writes

AS A Doctor I am often asked: "Doctor, given that you're responsible for wrongly administering chemotherapy to thousands of patients, how come you've still got your job?"

Well, the simple answer is that when a doctor is in trouble his problems are cured by other doctors using a treatment known as "Closing Ranks" or *Whitewashus Professionalis Normalis*, to give it the full medical name.

What happens with this treatment is that the doctor after a short period of time experiences no side effects such as loss of job or income, and soon begins to get well off again. The patients, on the other hand, feel extremely sick and irritable indeed.

If you are worried about feeling ill do NOT seek professional medical advice.

© A. Doctor

THAT PRESCOTT BOMBSHELL SPEECH IN FULL

by Our Labour Conference Staff **Lunchtime O'Mov**

"Brothers, sisters, comrades... great movement of ours... turning point... new dawn... forging links... hand in hand... fight and fight again... toilers by hand and by brain... Nye Bevan... grapefruit segments... bloody hell... come off it... Tory press... support John Smith... way forward... this great movement of ours... leopardskin accessories... vote for John Smith... mine's a Newcastle Brown *(standing ovation lasts several hours)*."

ON OTHER PAGES

Oratory Is Not Dead by Paul Johnson *6* Paul Johnson Is Dead Boring by Everyone Else *7* **Unfunny Omov Cartoon by Garland** *18*

IN THE COURTS

The Judicial Inquiry held by Mr Justice Scottlecarrot into the Iraqgate Affair

Day 94: The evidence of the Rt Dishonourable Mr David Mellor DJ, CD, NBG.

Miss Presley Emmerdale-Farm QC: Mr Mellor, I put it to you that you were a Minister of State in the Foreign Office in 1987.

Mellor: Yes, but I was far too senior to know what was going on.

Miss Elvis Presley: So you didn't know what was going on?

Mellor: I didn't say that. I knew exactly what was going on. I *am* a QC, you know, don't try any of your clever tricks with me.

Mr Justice Scottlecarrot: Kindly answer the question, please.

Mellor: I've forgotten what it was. I expect it was something pathetic about selling arms to Iraq.

Miss Drusilla Wensleydale: I put it to you again, Mr Mellor, that…

Mellor: Oh, for goodness sake, I'm a busy man. I've got an opera phone-in on Radio Haywards Heath in half an hour, and a piece to write for the *Guardian* on what it's like to be on an opera phone-in in Haywards Heath.

Miss Prunella Lymeswold: Mr Mellor, this is a serious business.

Mellor: Has anyone told you you're beautiful when you're angry? What are you doing after the hearing?

Mr Justice Scottlecarrot: Call Mr Waldegrave.

(Enter worried-looking man)

Waldegrave: Look, I've got it now. I've had many sleepless nights on this one, and I've worked out what to say. *(Pulls out piece of paper)* There was no change in our policy on selling arms to Iraq. If there had been a change, I would have announced it. And since I didn't announce it, there cannot have been a change. It is true that we changed the policy. But it was only a very slight change. One minute we said we wouldn't sell them arms. The next we said we would sell them arms.

Scottlecarrot: But surely, Mr Waldegrave, that is scarcely a small change?

Waldegrave: No, because if it had been a major change, I would have announced it.

Scottlecarrot: Then why didn't you announce it?

Waldenowingravetrouble: Because there would have been a huge row because it was such a major change.

Scottlecarrot: Mr Waldegrave, could you tell me how many apples there are in a picnic?

Waldegrave: I am innocent.

The hearing continues

School News

St Cakes

Goodman Term begins today. There are 285 boys in the school, 216 girls and 18 social workers. J.R.D. Quarter-Pounder (McDonald's) is Head of Nuggets. R.L.T. Burger-King (Garfunkel's) is Senior Mousemat. Miss Sunyatta Pizza-Hut (Wimpy's) is Day Vestal. The Headmaster Mr R.J.S. Spudulike, following a recent operation, wishes to be known in future as Ms Rowenta Spudulike. His wife Mrs Ethel Spudulike is standing by him, and will continue to teach Islamic Fundamentalist Studies to the Lower School. J.P. Drittsekk (Gummer's) will be Captain of the Runs, and Stools will be held on Frost's Bottom on 3 October. The School pop-group Cakes-R-Us will give a concert in the Old Oast on 4 November. The school play, *Jurassic Park*, will be performed in the Sega Room on 6 December. Tickets from the Bursar, Col. S.S. Demjanjuk, "Dunkillin". Takeaways will be on 23 December. The traditional carol service has been replaced by a celebration of Diwali, to be taken jointly by the Chaplain, Rev. Kevin Outreach, and Sri Lingam Bagwash O.C. (formerly Terence Nodes, Pilger's 1947-51).

The Alternative Rocky Horror Service Book

No. 94: A Service In Celebration Of A Parish Priest Who Wishes To Declare That He No Longer Believes In God.

The Bishop: Who is it that cometh forward as a clerk in holy orders to declare his unbelief?

Vicar: I do.

Bishop: That makes two of us.

All kneel for responses.

Bishop: O Lord, open thou our lips.

All: So that we can honestly and courageously declare that you don't exist.

Bishop: Let us pray.

All: Why?

Bishop: Alright, we'll leave that bit out.

All shall sit to hear the Vicar [Rev N. or M.] reciting the Non-Credo.

Vicar: I do not believe in God the Father, Almighty, nor in any of the rest of the rubbish. But I do believe in continuing to draw my salary, being written about in the *Daily Telegraph* and living in the Vicarage for ever and ever. Amen.

There shall then be sung some suitable hymn such as "Firmly I Don't Believe And Truly" from the New Age Traveller Hymn Book. During the hymn there will be a collection to enable the congregation to make up for the recent losses sustained by the Church Commissioners by contributing £800 million.

Bishop: Go in peace.

All: Thanks be to ourselves.

© Carey & Sharey Publications, in the Year Not Of Our Lord 1993.

BLIMEY! IT'S THE BLACK AND WHITE MARRIAGE SHOW

by Our Man At The Front
GARRY BUSHELL

GUESS who's coming to dinner, Rupert?! YOU, probably, in your new son-in-law's cooking pot! 'Cos your nearest and dearest has only just gone and got herself hitched to someone from Bongo-Bongo Land! Elkin Pianim, no less! Bloody Elkin! Excuse my Ghanaian!! Couldn't she find any decent Aussies, Yanks or Brits without ending up shacking up with one of our African cousins!?!

Coming over here and stealing our women!?! Blimey! Still, loved the dress — pity it was the groom's father who was wearing it!?!

Blimey! Rupert, what are you giving him for a wedding present? A banjo?!? And what are the guests getting? Watermelon? Blimey!
(You're fired. R.M.)

"No, I said he was a Dirty **Digger**!"

⬤ THAT MURDOCH WEDDING — AS SEEN IN THE SUN

ROYAL WEDDING MAKES WORLD REJOICE

by Our Court Staff
O.B.N. LICKSPITTLEJOHN

ALL OVER the world bells rang out last night to celebrate the historic union of two great cultures, shining a beacon of hope across the globe. Her Royal Highness Elizabeth, the heir to the Murdoch throne, was wed in solemn grandeur to St Elkin Pianim, the son of the Ghanaian Ashanti Chieftain, A. Kwame Pianim.

The peoples of the world danced openly in the streets as the epoch-shattering nuptials were celebrated from the Sun to Today, from the Times to the Sunday Times *(shurely 'from Sydney to San Francisco'? Ed)*.

Messages of goodwill poured in from heads of department from all over Murdoch's empire and, as the radiant couple were wafted away on a honeymoon in heaven, peace broke out all over the universe.

God bless you, King Rupert! And may I have a rise? *(Shurely 'May choirs of angels sing thee to thy rest'? Ed.)*

The Daily Hellograph

FRIDAY, OCTOBER 8, 1993

Huge Shake-Up At Radio One

The 'Night of the Long Waves'

By Our Home Affairs Staff
D.J. TAYLOR, D.J. ENRIGHT AND D.J. THRIBB

BY FAR the most important event yesterday, our marketing department informs us, was the extraordinary announcement that Simon Beard, 58, and Alan Hairpiece, 61, are to be replaced as presenters of Radio One's prestigious shows, *Good Morning Pop Pickers* and *Good Afternoon Pop Pickers*.

This follows the shock "on air" resignation of Dave Tee Shirt, 74, the presenter of the popular late-night programme, *Good Evening Pop Pickers*.

The exit of BBC One's "top three" represents the biggest earthquake in British broadcasting since Lord Reith stepped down in 1846.

Zimmer Holiday

The new controller of Radio One is to be 21-year-old Gary Pimple, who first sprang to fame today when he emerged from obscurity to become Controller of Radio One.

Pimple is determined to stop the steady decline in Radio One's audiences which has been continuous since 1967.

He says: "Radio One is the jewel in our flagship. We will not allow it to be eroded by the likes of Richard Branson's Radio Mates FM and Radio Haywards Heath."

How It Will Look — Radio One's New Line-Up

7-10am Steve Zitt, 15, with The New Big Toast Breakfast Show.

10am-3pm Zena Glitter, 27, presents The Best of Zangra, Techno and Dub Bubble.

3-4pm The Marty Smartie Laugh Hour, featuring TV's Marty Smartie.

4-7pm David Mellor presents some of his favourite hits on CD.

7pm-Midnight John Peel, 76, presents the No One's Listening Show.

Close Down.

Report and picture — P14

Miss Koo Stark To Marry Another Man

By Our Court and Social Correspondent QUENTIN LETCH

THE society photographer Miss Kooala ("Koo") Stark is to marry again, it was announced today.

Miss Stark, 27, was formerly linked with a number of libel actions (*shurely 'men including HRH the Duke of York'? M.H.*)

Max most popular boy's name

By Our News Staff
LUNCHTIME O'B.N.

THE SECOND most important event of yesterday, according to our editor, was the annual survey of boy's names, showing that Max is the most popular name given to children by members of the *Daily Hellograph* staff.

THAT LIST IN FULL

Max	14
Conrad	12
Barbara	3
W.F.	2
TV's Charles	1

Peregrine, once the most popular name, this year dropped out of the list altogether for the first time.

New-Look Easy To Solve Hellograph Crossword Puzzle
(set by our Marketing Department)

Across

1. Mad anon (anagram).

Prize: 2 tickets to Madonna concert.

LATE NEWS

Fascist Wins At Isle of Dogs

Mr Conrad Blackshirt, 56, today romped home in the *Daily Hellograph* "Most Popular Proprietor" competition. "I am not a fascist — I am Napoleon," he told waiting psychiatrists.

ON OTHER PAGES
□ Leader — Whither Popular Radio? 18 □ W.F. Deedes — Has It All Gone Too Far? 19 □ Paul Johnson — Why Oh Why Can't They Bring Back Jimmy Savile? 18

EMPEROR'S NEW COLLECTION WOWS FASHION WORLD

Milan, Tuesday

THERE were gasps around the catwalk yesterday as the Emperor revealed his new clothes to a stunned audience in his sensational new Autumn show.

Called the "See Through" collection and starting at $57 million per item, the new couture drew plaudits from the assembled fashion critics.

"Quite brilliant," said *Vogue*'s Nikki Coleridge; "Wonderful," said *Harpers*' Vikki Noods; "Can I have all the advertising to put in my magazine, please?" said all the other editors.

Everyone agreed that the clothes really are dazzling with a totally original approach to fabric, er... colour, er... design, er... well, you know, they are the Emperor's, they must be marvellous.

"Women everywhere will want to wear my clothes," said the Emperor. "They are incredibly versatile and practical and yet they are still the ultimate fashion statement."

Waif your money goodbye

There was a minor incident at the Palazzo Contricciano when a small boy in the crowd suggested to the Emperor that he did not have any new clothes at all.

The boy was shouted down by the assembled designers, experts, buyers, supermodels, journalists, celebrities. Said one silly woman with too much money: "If the Emperor is not a genius, I'll eat this invisible hat I've just bought from him."

Kate Moss is 11-7-9.

That new Pinter play text in full

(Middleaged man in glasses sitting in room. Critic enters nervously)

Pinter: Did you like my play?

(Very long pause indeed)

"Morning, Vicar"

HUGE JOB LOSSES IN CIVIL SERVICE AS CLARKE WIELDS AXE

by our Whitehall **Lunchtime O'Fficial**

MILLIONS of civil servants are not to lose their jobs as the Government plans the biggest ever reduction in public spending.

But Whitehall will not be exempt as billions of pounds are wiped off spending on the Health Service, the armed forces, public transport and single parent mothers (*Don't you just hate them?* © P. Lilley, M. Portillo etc.)

It was announced that there will be a savage cut of no less than one job in the whole of Whitehall. Mr Malcolm Velcro, 58, an Assistant Deputy Controller in the Filing Cabinet and Clipboard Inspectorate of the Department of Overmanning, is to take early retirement in 1998.

"Make no mistake about it," said Mr Kenneth Clarke yesterday, "there will be blood on the carpet as I get really tough with these bureaucrats."

Late last night, however, Mr Velcro announced that he had appealed to the Clipboard Appeals Tribunal presided over by Mr Justice Velcro (relation) who found that the decision to make Mr Velcro redundant was "a vicious and totally unwarranted attack on a vital public service".

Mr Clarke immediately accepted the judge's ruling, announcing that Mr Velcro had been reinstated with an increase in salary of 16.4 per cent.

The saving, he explained, would easily be made by laying off another 2,500 nurses and disbanding the Somerset, Hampshire and Staffordshire Armoured Light Infantry Artillery Battalion.

The Memoirs

For millions of years God has kept quiet about what really went on behind the clouds. But now, at last, in his eagerly awaited memoirs, the Supreme Ruler of the Universe reveals himself as never before in a series of frank assessments of some of those who were closest to him during his millions of years in power — from the early days when he formed the world to the present day, when no one believes in him any more.

Howe are the mighty fallen

The Day Lucifer Betrayed Me

I ALWAYS had a high regard for Lucifer and promoted him to Archangel very shortly after the beginning of time. He had many outstanding qualities, and handled the Creation Portfolio with great skill and

Adam: a few apples short of a Tree of Knowledge

diplomacy. He was, however, ambitious — which I always saw as something of a flaw in a senior member of the Host. As time went on, Lucifer came to believe that he was indispensable, a dangerous failing in any eternal being.

I remember he came to me shortly after we produced our first White Paper on the creation of the Garden of Eden Development. He told me then that he wanted to be known as Deputy God, and demanded additional Seraphim to attend him at his celestial dwelling.

I was astonished, as he was already perfectly well supplied with seraphim, cherubim, thrones, dominions and powers.

He was plainly disappointed when I initially turned down his request, although, in order to mollify him, I agreed to a further meeting on Cloud Nine later in that Millennium. Imagine my amazement when I heard that he had appeared at a mass meeting of

angels to explain that he had resigned from my service.

He then launched out on an extraordinary speech, full of bile and treachery. He said that he had for a long time been finding it increasingly difficult to support my policies — in particular the so-called Ten Commandments.

Using the analogy of the game of cricket, which I had not yet invented, he said that working for me was "like a batsman being told by his captain to bowl googlies with his pads on".

The traitor ended by inviting all his fellow archangels to "consider their positions", which was a clear incitement to revolt.

I told him that, if that was

what he thought, he could "go to hell" — which he promptly did. It was a sad end to our long working partnership, and a sorry conclusion to a promising career in heavenly life.

The Day I Was Betrayed By Adam

MANY people said at the time that I was quite wrong to give my backing to Adam, whom I had created from nothing at an early stage in my administration.

They were quite wrong. In the beginning Adam did everything I told him, and was plainly head and shoulders above the beasts of the field.

Aware that he needed to gain administrative experience, I put Adam in charge of naming the animals — "cat", "dog", "giraffe", "bastard".

When I saw this, I said it was good. It was only later that I was to be sadly disillusioned by Adam, when he became flagrantly disobedient to my will and began to flout my orders.

What became known as the "Gardengate" episode was the turning point. Adam had begun to drift intellectually, and was floating with the liberal tide.

He fell under the influence of advisers such as Norman Serpent. And, when he fell for the wiles of the so-called "Euro-snake", I realised that he had let me down in the most treacherous fashion.

He was weak, vacillating and not up to the job. Typically, when things began to go wrong, he tried to put the blame on his wife and the media.

He even claimed that my years in power had not been a "golden age" at all. He told everyone that he was his "own man". It was a very sad end to a promising career in heavenly life.

NEXT WEEK: Lord Noah — what a washout. Moses — hopeless. Abraham — weak-willed. Job — a whinger.

© Harper-Gnome 1993.

God: No one measured up

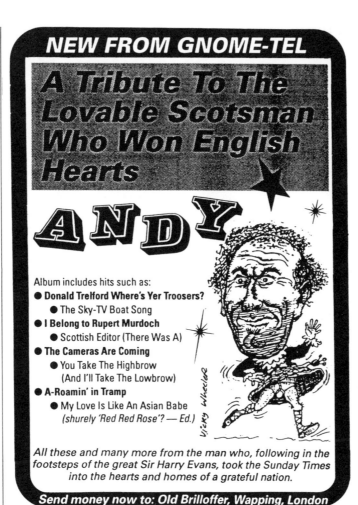

NEW FROM GNOME-TEL

A Tribute To The Lovable Scotsman Who Won English Hearts

ANDY

Album includes hits such as:
- **Donald Trelford Where's Yer Troosers?**
  - The Sky-TV Boat Song
- **I Belong to Rupert Murdoch**
  - Scottish Editor (There Was A)
- **The Cameras Are Coming**
  - You Take The Highbrow (And I'll Take The Lowbrow)
- **A-Roamin' in Tramp**
  - My Love Is Like An Asian Babe *(shurely 'Red Red Rose'? — Ed.)*

Vicky Wheeler

All these and many more from the man who, following in the footsteps of the great Sir Harry Evans, took the Sunday Times into the hearts and homes of a grateful nation.

Send money now to: Old Brilloffer, Wapping, London

POETRY CORNER

In Memoriam
Andy Stewart

So farewell then
Andy Stewart
Of White Heather
Club fame.

Keith's Mum
Says that New
Year will never
Be the same
Again.

"Should auld acquaintance
Be forgot?"

Not in
Your case
We hope.

E.J. McThribb (17½)

This poem is being entered for the prestigious £5,000 T.S. Eliot Award and will be reprinted in the Independent along with some that are even worse.

"We do, however, have an alternative to burial or cremation"

NO ONE KILLED FOR FIVE MINUTES

by Our Northern Ireland Correspondent **Sir Patrick Mayhem**

THERE was renewed tension in the province yesterday when no one was murdered for a space of five minutes. Spokesmen for extremists on both sides condemned the non-violence as a worrying sign and paramilitaries from both the Republican and Protestant wings were quick to deny responsibility for the lack of atrocities. They said that there would be "renewed efforts to re-start the violence" as soon as possible.

TV Highlights

THE AVENGERS They're back! That man in the bowler hat with the orange sash and his violent sidekicks meting our their own brand of justice. First seen in the 'sixties, this "hit" series has continued ever since with its popular blend of mindless violence and violent mindlessness. Attracts fanatical following. *(Bloody Repeat)*

THE STAGE NOVEMBER 5 1993   page 94

SAMMY SPOONS
Cabaret entertainer, ventriloquist and balloon artist. As seen on Anglia TV's talent show "Don't Call Us". Available for panto, children's parties, RSC etc.

FRANKIE FAME
Known as
The Golden Voice.
Fresh from a season on the P&O *Spirit of Bruges* ferry (Sheerness to Ostend). Sings light classical to country and western. Supported Kennie Sanders Jazz Band on recent Belgian tour.

'GERRY'
Soundalike Irishman with uncanny Gerry Adams vocal impersonation!! He even does lip-sync! You'll believe it's really Mr Sinn Fein himself! But you won't believe what he's saying!! As seen on 9 O'Clock News, News at Ten, Newsnight, Channel 4 News etc. Available for Peace Talks, Apologies, IRA Funerals, Political Blackmail etc.
Will bring own onion.

That New-Look Rolling Radio 5
What You Will Hear

...and it's Pevsner in the number 5 shirt looking dangerous in front of goal... the Dollis Hill back four are standing like statues... there's Gary Gebler-Davies in the sweeper role... he's about to shoot and it's...

Newscaster: It's 3.47 and time to go over to our Foreign News Desk for a newsflash.

Reporter: And the news here in Athens is that Masoch may be about to pull of an extraordinary election coup. With only seven weeks to go before polling day, an opinion poll shows the former President Slapandtiklos 14 points ahead of his main rival, Col. Stassinopoulos...

Announcer: And now, before the weather forecast and traffic news, we go over to Kingston, Jamaica, for an update on the 3rd Test.

Brian Johnson: We welcome Radio 5 listeners to Test Match Special with the news that I have just been sent this delicious cannabis cake by a local listener, Mrs Rasta Fairyann. And it's a huge pink elephant taking the new ball at the pavilion end and... hold on... I think it's a flying saucer hovering just over square leg...

Announcer: It's 3.52 and time for another rolling newsflash from Brussels.

Reporter: Where the news is that the latest Council of Ministers' decision on the GATT round is that farm support prices in the sheepmeat sector may have to be reduced by another 21.6 per cent if agreement is to be reached at the crucial Geneva meeting next month.

Announcer: And now, at 3.54, we've just got time to pick up the latest score from the Australian Windsurfing Championships in Perth...

Australian Voice: And the Chinese team this year have really taken everyone by surprise. The women are particularly strong in all classes, especially the Synchronised Freestyle...

Announcer: And now, at 3.56, we've just got time before the News and Sport headlines at 4 o'clock for details of what you can hear on BBC Radio in the next hour.

Another Announcer: Radio Four is about to split into two wavebands. On FM you will hear nothing at all, except crackles. On Long Wave at 4.00 you can hear Children's Hour, which used to be here on Radio Five, now retitled Children's Five Minutes. Then, at 4.05, we have a repeat of last Tuesday's Does He Take Precautions?, the safe sex programme for the disabled community introduced by Libby Glibby, and a look ahead at what's on this evening's Radio Three.

Natalie Wheen: Hullo. On Radio Three this evening we shall be having a series of highlights from Classic FM, and at 9.45 the first full-length interview with the contemporary Polish composer Waldemar Ignatieff...

Announcer: And now, before the news headlines, we've just got time for a newsflash from the Radio Five Rolling Media Staff.

Reporter: And the news from here at Broadcasting House is that the BBC is going to launch a new network, Radio Six, which will consist entirely of complaints from listeners about what a balls-up we've made of all the other networks...

(Continued on 94 KHz FM and 994 KHz LW indefinitely)

Bethlehem Star

Editor: Charles Myrrh

Now only 20 Shekels

Storm grows over lone mothers

by Frankincense Johnson

PHARISEES and politicians joined forces last night to condemn the wave of single parenthood which has been sweeping Bethlehem in recent days.

Ministers have linked the increase in so-called "lone mums" with the rising tide of crime which has lately been rocking Judaea.

"It is time to return to basic family values," said the Emperor Notveryaugustus (formerly Johannus Minimus) and he was strongly supported by his henchmen Pontius Portillo and Petrus Lillius.

Don't Consider The Lilley

One opponent of single motherhood went even further. Michael Herod, the Judaean Interior Minister, pointed to recent research which showed that all first-born children without fathers "lacked a proper role model" and would almost certainly "succumb to peer pressure" by becoming hardened criminals.

"My solution is simple," said Howard. "All first-born children should be slaughtered immediately and that will bring an end to crime."

Backing Mr Herod's call for tough action, the Pharisees stressed the importance of the two-parent family in both Jewish and Roman life.

They cited a particularly distressing example of a young unmarried mother who had actually come to Bethlehem in order to jump the queue for accommodation.

"She had come from her home in the country and was immediately given a stable of her own, complete with manger, swaddling clothes, oxen, asses and other benefits."

Blessed Are The Portillo

The Pharisees continued: "The moral character of this woman can be judged by the fact that in the days after her son was born, she entertained a continual stream of male visitors, ranging from rough shepherds to wealthy foreigners, some of them coloured, bringing exotic substances into the home."

Neighbours were deafened by the persistent playing of loud music, and light shows in the sky.

"How can we possibly expect a child brought up in such circumstances," the Pharisees concluded, "to grow up into a useful member of society? Mark our words, this youngster will end up on the wrong side of the law and no mistake. It would not surprise us to see him in 33 years time being nailed up."

ON OTHER PAGES

"*Gerry Adams didn't say anything today, but his gestures are performed by a mime artist*"

Booker winners

Kenneth Clarke Ha Ha Ha

Hilarious story of boy with mental age of ten who finds it difficult to add up.

Paddy Ashdown Ha Ha Ha

Hilarious story of boy of 10 seats who says he is going to form the next government and then crashes his car.

Alan Clark Ha Ha Ha

Hilarious story of boy of 10 women who refuses to appear in front of the Scott Inquiry.

Roddy Doyle Ha Ha ha

Hilarious story of man laughing all the way to the bank. (*That's enough. Ed*)

WORLD EXCLUSIVE

SEXY DAVE IN SECRET PIX STORM

THIS is one of the sensational secret pictures the world is crying out not to see. It shows Mirror Editor David Banks sweating away on the publicity machine and losing thousands of pounds in the process.

Dave believes in keeping fat. He joined the exclusive Holborn Fatness Centre in a bid to improve his circulation and develop his figure (2.57 million and falling).

But we don't print this photograph merely out of prurience. It is not just an excuse to show photographs of a semi-naked fat man with his chequebook wide open.

We publish the Banks pictures for three very good reasons.

1) Firstly, out of deep love and respect for one of the finest editors on Fleet Street.

2) If that won't wash, how about: secondly, because the pictures prove at last that Mr Banks is *not* suffering from any slimming disease and is currently as enormously overweight as he ever was.

3) Er... well, OK, you didn't believe those two — but this reason is a cracker: the pictures highlight an issue of national security. Mr Banks edits a national whose future is far from secure.

WE SAY
WE ♥ FATSO!

That Upperclass Blind Date in full —
Hooray Henry and Sloane fail to hit it off

Cilla: You've been all over the world on holiday and you had a sooper wedding in St Paul's Cathedral and you gorra a beautiful home in Gloucestershire and yer own helicopter thrown in. So tell us, chuck, did yer 'ave a luvly time?

Prince Charles *(for it is he)*: Yes, it was very agreeable to begin with, we had a lot of fun especially when we went to Spain and stayed with the King.

Cilla: Ooh, posh! *(Audience cheer)* Now what about you, luv, did yer 'ansome prince turn out like you hoped?

Princess Diana *(for it is she)*: Well, Cilla, to be honest, I think I picked the wrong one. Charles is much older than me and very serious. In fact, he's a bit of a bore.

Cilla: Ooh!!

(Shot of red-faced Charles on sofa next to Di looking very angry)

Charles: That really is appalling. Just because I play polo and the cello, talk about architecture and Shakespeare and the meaning of life and so forth doesn't mean I'm boring.

Cilla: Quite right, chuck! Come off it, Di, he's a lovely fella, isn't he everyone?

(Audience cheer wildly and wave flags)

Charles: Thank you. Thank you very much indeed. You're very kind.

Cilla: And 'ow did the pair of youse gerron social-like?

Diana: He didn't like any of my friends.

Charles: And she didn't like mine either, particularly Camilla.

Diana: And what about Squidgie then?

Cilla: Now, now you two. You sound just like a married couple! *(Audience has hysterics at Cilla's familiar joke from the autocue)* Will youse be seeing each other again or is tharrit?

Charles: Well, I'm perfectly happy to meet now and again, at the Trooping The Colour and that sort of thing.

Cilla: Well, Di, he still wants to see ya, so there's still hope, eh wack?

Diana: No, there bloody well isn't.

(Audience cheers wildly)

Cilla: Well, that's it for now. Next week it's the oldies' turn. Lovely Raine Spencer and the suave Count de Chambrun. We'll be seeing how they got on on their… BLIND DATE! Tarra!!!

(Silly music and caption rolls)

COMING SOON: *Oliver Reed and Jeff Bernard go out together in BLIND DRUNK.*

Wedding of the Century – How They Are Related

Food Minister Nicholas Soames

Serena Smith

Nicholas Soames line	John Smith line
Eddie The Large	John Smith Ye Smith
Ethelred The Enormous	W.H. Smith Ye Newsreader
Henry The Seconds	John Smith Ye Crispmaker
Richard The Thirds	Mel Smith Ye Telecom Share Salesman
Sir Thomas More-Please	John Smith Ye Leader of the Labour Party
1st Lard of the Admiralty	John Smith's Fruity Daughters
The Marlboro Man	The Smiths (featuring Morrisey)
Sir Winston Filter-Tips-Churchill	Joan Smith (as seen on TV)
Sir Matrix Churchill	Serena Scot (not much seen on TV)
Soames from The Forsyte Saga	Selena Smith
Fatty Soames	Stan Smith
Even Fattier Soames	**Serena Stanhope**
Pavarotti	

 Progress

1991: Mirror run by Fat Idiot.   **1992:** Mirror run by Banks.   **1993:** Mirror run by Fat Idiot called Banks.

CHARLES OF ARABIA

THE STORY SO FAR: The Prince of Wales has flown to Kuwait as part of his mission to rebuild his public image.

Now read on…

C HARLES'S camel snorted furiously as the Royal Party neared the crest of Shawaddi Waddi, the great sand dune from where they could see the ancient tomb of Princess Al Lin Baba, the wisest and most beautiful of the daughters of the Wazir of Strobes.

"Hold her firm, Your Highness," instructed the trusty camelman Sharif. "The camel she is like a beautiful woman. You must always show her who is in control."

How true that was, Charles thought, how very true when you thought about it. If only he had kept a tighter rein on Diana then perhaps everything would not have been so appalling. Because it really was appalling when you thought about it. But there was no point in dwelling on the past. As his old friend and mentor, Sir Laurens van der Post had put it in his book *I Did It My Way: Travels Through Life*: "Pack up your troubles in your old kit bag and smile, smile, smile."

How very true that was as well. Everything seemed so true here in the pure air of the desert.

He drew alongside the Exxon of Kuwait who smiled, revealing his white and gold teeth. "Yes, my brother, the desert, she is like a beautiful woman. She stretches out before us with her valleys and dunes asking us to explore her."

"Yes, indeed," said Charles as the Exxon nudged him in the ribs with his white rhino horn camel whip. What an impressive figure the Exxon was, he thought, with his ornate Bedouin headdress and single-breasted silk Yamani suit. He was the epitome, thought Charles, of the modern monarch, combining the traditions of a noble past with a command of the contemporary world. Sunglasses and camels. Rolex watch and abacus. Yes! This would be himself before long, he decided, in his new incarnation. The gutter press trivialities would be forgotten, Diana would be confined to the sidelines and, like the Exxon, he, Charles, would rescue

his country and become a symbol of unity between all the warring thingies and so on. He could see it all…

After they had travelled a few more miles, the Exxon asked: "Would you like to fly my kestrel? Her name is Squijji."

"Er… Yes… Thank you," said Charles, gingerly holding out his arm as the Exxon expertly placed a magnificent hooded bird onto his wrist. The creature immediately sank her talons deep into Charles's Reeves and Mortimer tropical jacket. He let out an involuntary cry of pain. The Exxon smiled: "The kestrel is like a beautiful woman. You must put a bag over head to keep her quiet."

Charles felt that this was rather less

true than some of the other things the Exxon had said, but he nodded vigorously nonetheless.

The faithful Sharif removed the leather hood from the bird and at once the kestrel flew off into the azure blue, never to be seen again.

THE picnic lunch at the Salman Oasis lived up to Charles's expectations. As they walked through the luscious gardens where tinkling fountains played and palm trees extended their fronds to create an Elysian shade, a sumptuous banquet had been prepared for the party of thirty princes. In the middle of a ceremonial Asilnadir rug sat a huge plate groaning with sheep's eyes. The Exxon invited him to begin.

"You are hungry, Your Highness. This is our finest Arab delicacy."

Charles forced himself to swallow the glutinous mass that had once graced the visage of a proud desert ram.

"Are you not joining me, Your Highness?" Charles gulped as he noticed that the Exxon was not eating.

"Oh no. They are all for you. I will have a Big Mac later, at the Palace. I find that food is like a beautiful woman. You have to wait a bit and then she comes out nice and hot..."

The other princes squatting in a circle along with Charles all nodded, but then the mood seemed to change from one of proverbial wisdom to what Charles could only describe as lewd gaiety. He was amazed to see a copy of the *Sunday Mirror* being passed avidly between the princelings. And there was Prince Fatwa thrusting his clenched fist in the air to the accompaniment of lascivious grunts. At once he saw, spreadeagled across the front page of the paper, his estranged wife, clad only in a leotard.

The Exxon handed Charles the paper and sniggered. "Your wife, she is like a beautiful woman..."

Charles suddenly felt his lunch churning in his stomach. Was there no length to which Diana would not go to keep herself in the public eye? The very thought of the word 'eye' made him feel even more nauseous. And, clutching his stomach, he ran behind the nearest palm tree, leaving behind the mocking laughter of the sons of the desert.

(To be continued)

WEATHER

Poetry Corner

Lines on the Retirement of D.I. Gower from First Class Cricket

So, Farewell
Then.

David Gower.

You are too
Old to
Play cricket

For England.

And too
Good.

A Nation
Mourns.

E.J. Thribb 17½ (Retired)

This poem by E.J. Thribb has been shortlisted for the Pipesucker Prize (£10.25p) and comes from his latest collection, "More Dead Leaves". Thribb hopes it is sufficiently bad to be reprinted in the *Independent*.

THE CONTROVERSIAL VOICE

Every week **Dave Spart**, *Co-Chair of Docklands Anti-Racist-Hunt-Saboteur-End-Student-Sexual-Harassment Alliance, looks at the issues behind the news.*

The totally sickening police brutality marred an otherwise peaceful protest march against the BNP fascist scum and in particular the so-called councillor Derek Goebbels showing once again the secret conspiracy that exists er... between the Nazis in the police force and their confreres within the judiciary not to mention the right-wing media which typically distorted the true events in an effort to show that the violence was entirely perpetrated by left-wing demonstrators against the police which it was er... but the presence of black policemen deliberately sent as a provocative gesture by the establishment inflamed the protesters and diverted them from their legal and peaceful aim of setting fire to the BNP bookshop and killing all the people in it er ... as Lenin wrote

(cont p.94)

"They certainly try and give value for money these days"

EDWARD SETS UP AS INDEPENDENT TEA PRODUCER

(shurely 'TV'? Ed)

by Our Media Staff **P.G. Tips**

THE WORLD of hot beverages *(shurely 'television'? Ed)* was rocked to its foundations yesterday by the news that Prince Edward, the fifth in line to the throne of England, is to create his own independent company which will produce highbrow tea *(shurely 'TV programmes including factual current affairs and arts documentaries'? Ed)* for sale to the network.

Prince Edward brings a wide range of technical knowledge to his new job, having produced a large amount of tea *(don't you mean 'theatre'? Ed)* for Andrew Lloyd Webber at the Really Useful Company, getting rave reviews such as "Mmm", "Oooh", and "Delicious" in his brief time there.

Said a spokesman: "He's got a very good eye for a cuppa and his years of experience stirring, adding milk and disposing of unwanted teabags will be a real plus in the future." Said another: "He has always been interested in variety: Earl Grey, Lapsang Souchong, Ceylon, Breakfast Mix — even mint tea. There's very little, tea-wise, that Edward can't turn his hand to."

Edward will eschew any formal titles at the new company, and will be known simply as "Boy".

(That's quite enough of this piece. Ed)

Yes! It's 20th Century American Art at the Royal Academy Rhyming Slang

Edward Hopper	**Show stopper**
Man Ray	**Seen enough today**
Willem de Kooning	**Pseuds are swooning**
Frank Stella	**Forget it, fella**
Ellsworth Kelly	**One for George Melly**
Jasper Johns	**More cons**
Jeff Koons	**King of the loons**
Liechtenstein	**The bubble's fine**
Rothko	**Time to go**
Jackson Pollock	**This stuff's not very good**

(That's enough slang. Ed)

The Daily Hellograph

A Time To Be Serious

A VISITOR from outer space might easily conclude from a study of the British press in recent days that the most important event on the entire surface of the globe was the publication by the Daily Mirror of a series of photographs showing the Princess of Wales engaged in aerobic exercises at a London gymnasium. How have we reached a situation where a happening of such essential triviality and miniscule import can be presented on every side as an occurrence of almost cosmic significance?

Day after day there is comment, analysis, reportage and pontification in an endless stream. And yet, while the attention of millions of readers is focussed on all the tedious ramifications of the so-called "Gymgate Affair", an infinitely more important and tragic event is unfolding in our country, and is receiving almost no attention from the Fourth Estate.

We refer, of course, to the outrageous treatment of Mr Jeremy Paxman at the hands of the anonymous "blackballers" of the Garrick Club. Surely this country and indeed our entire civilisation has reached the bottom of the pit when one of our most distinguished communicators can be treated like a social leper by the most important institution known to man. O Tempora, O Mores.

Also in today's Hellograph

New Competition From The Marketing Department

Now you too can be put up for London's most exclusive club.

Just collect 84 tokens from the Daily Telegraph and complete the following sentence: I am giving up reading the Telegraph because it's full of rubbish about the Garrick Club . . . .

NAME . . . .

ADDRESS . . . .

HOUSE OF COMMONS
OFFICIAL REPORT

PARLIAMENTARY DEBATES

HANZ-Z-Z-ARD

The Triumphant Return of Mr Michael Heseltarzan, Westminster's Wittiest Man.

3.15 pm

Sir Bufton Tufton (Lymeswold, Con): May I, on behalf of this whole House, record our very deep pleasure in welcoming back the President of the Board of Trade, Sir Winston Heseltine? *[Prolonged cheering, chant of "For Hezza jolly good fellow"]*

Mr Robin Cook (Beard-under-Chin, Lab): Will the President kindly explain why all the coal mines he promised to reprieve are now being closed down?

Mr Heseltine (Westland, Con): With the honourable member, it always seems to be a case of "too many cooks spoiling the Labour Party". *[Hysterical laughter continues for several minutes, cries of "Hezza's back", "It's the way you tell 'em", and "You're so funny you'll give us a heart attack"]*

Mr Cook: I repeat the question — why is the coal industry being systematically murdered by this uncaring, hypocritical government?

Mr Heseltine: Who won the last election then? Once a Socialist, always a Socialist, that's what I say. If you lot were in, things would be even worse than they are. *[Explosion of laughter blows roof off Commons and continues for several hours]*

Mr Creepy Backbencher (Flattery, Con): Could the greatest prime minister of modern times please be kind enough to tell us what is in his diary?

John Major (Fifty-and-three-quarters, Con): I would refer the honourable member to page 94 of this magazine.

Mr Heseltine: And here's another one, folks. How many members of the Labour Party does it take to change a light bulb? *[Cries of "Answer, answer"]*

Mrs Betty Booproyd, Speaker: Will the President of the Board of Trade please answer his own question?

Mr Heselwit: The answer — wait for it — is none. Because the Labour Party never changes anything! *[Whole nation expires with mirth]*

TO PLAY THE FOOL

THE STORY SO FAR: Charles is spending the long winter nights watching a new television series.

Now read on…

"IT REALLY is appalling." The actor playing the King of England was talking to his prime minister about the proposed redevelopment of Victoria Street.

Charles was sitting alone in the Lycett Green drawing room at Highgrove, staring at his new 42in Haritomsun quadraphonic TV screen, a present from the Crown Prince of Sinatra in recognition of the good work he had done in arranging the sale of two Budgie anti-personnel helicopters.

Charles still felt strange sitting there on his own — the shelves now empty of Diana's beloved videos, the vacant space over the mantelpiece where once had hung the signed photo of her and Phil Collins. Was that his name? How long ago it all seemed — a world now irrevocably lost.

As he sat there in the darkened room the words of his old friend and mentor Sir Laurens van der Post came back to comfort him. "Time, my boy, is a great healer," as he had once said to him by the campfire, in the great Redhead Forests of the Kalahari. How very true that was, Charles mused, and how very untrue this silly play was.

Now there was a scene of the King striding along a gravel path at Buckingham Palace talking to the prime minister in a silly voice.

"You see, what I want is a sort of, er, role thingie. There's so much to be done. You know, the inner cities, the environment, er, Shakespeare, that sort of thing."

"Quite so," the prime minister was replying. "But it wouldn't do, Your Majesty, to be too controversial. I'll see what I can do."

Charles was getting impatient. Why could these television chaps never get anything right?

"I mean, that fellow could never be King," he exclaimed, "with his ridiculous voice and absurd mannerisms. No one could take him seriously. He'd be a laughing stock."

Charles looked back at the screen. Now the King was sitting in a sauna bath while his attractive young ethnic affairs adviser Miss Fatima Wandulu told him what he should say at the Annual Banquet of the Worshipful Company of Moneylenders and Usurers.

"You must tell them, Sire, to launch a new multi-cultural awareness programme inside Britain's major corporations."

"Yes, yes," said the actor playing the King, as he dried himself with a towel. "It's like my old friend and mentor sir Clarence van der Valk always says: 'People who need people are the luckiest people in the world.'"

Charles leaped to his feet and called for Sir Alan Fitztightly. "Turn this rubbish off, will you!" he demanded, and immediately the pink-cardiganed figure of his equerry shimmered from the darkness and, with one deft movement of the remote control, the screen went silent.

"There you are, my dear. Are you sure you didn't want to watch the snooker on the other side?"

"No." Charles grimaced. "I've seen enough television. It really is appalling…"

"IT REALLY is appalling." Charles was striding purposefully along the gravel path in the gardens of Buckingham Palace. In the distance he could see the famous fountain by Alessandro Mussolini, The Triumph of Fascism, which his great-uncle the Duke of Windsor, had been given on his visit to the Vatican in 1929.

The grey-suited figure of the prime minister at his side struggled to keep up.

"Oh yes," he agreed. "What exactly was it, sir, that was appalling?"

Charles turned to John Major and explained patiently, his features creasing in exasperation.

"You see, I haven't got a proper role. I feel I could contribute so much more than I do. It's all very well these inner cities and environment thingies — but I really should be getting involved at the sharp end, you know, business, exports, that kind of thing."

"Quite so," coughed the deferential prime minister. "But with respect, sir, you must consider your constitutional position. And what would your mother say?"

GARY ANDREWS 1993

"That's alright, she's dead," Charles replied in a dreamy voice.

The prime minister reeled back in shock.

"What's that, sir? Are you sure?"

Charles snapped out of his momentary reverie with a sense of profound embarrassment.

"Oh dear," he said, "I must have been thinking about something else. I'm very jetlagged. I've been in Kuwait selling all these exports. Flying the flag. Very tiring."

Charles was interrupted by his new adviser on Multi-Environmental issues, Wanda Sarfraz.

"I'm sorry to interrupt you, sir," said the attractive young Asian girl, as she caught up with the two men next to a large bed of winter-flowering Camillas, "but we really have got to finish that speech you're giving in the City tonight to the Worshipful Company of Offshoremen and Tax Avoiders. I thought you could say something about the new initiative for multi-…"

Charles suddenly felt overcome by an extraordinary sense of deja-vu. What was it that the old Indian sage Shri Hari Sikkom had said? "Life repeats itself, first as a rotten old TV play, then as reality itself." No, that couldn't be it.

A skein of Canada Dry geese flew overhead, on their way to their winter breeding ground at Canary Wharf. They screamed demonically.

The New Rocky Horror NATIVITY PLAY

For use in all schools at the end of December (formerly Christmas)

(Curtain rises to show Mary and Youssef arriving at the DSS offices)

Youssef: I want to register a complaint. My partner is pregnant and we have been denied accommodation because we are of Afro-Caribbean, Asian or other ethnic origin.

Official: Oh dear, that certainly sounds like one for the Commission for Racial Equality.

(The cast shall here sing the traditional carol: "O come all ye multi-faithful")

Official: But first we have a statutory obligation to provide you with board and lodging for the night. Could you just fill in these forms and then we have a happy ending to the story.

As the couple sign the forms, all shall sing:

"Away in a Mecca
Where Mohammed was
                           born
Muslims are celebrating
This happy morn.
The same is true of Buddha
And Little Lord Krishna too
Not forgetting the Sikhs
              and Rastafarians,
They all have their own
perfectly valid religious
                         view."

(Enter sour-faced person of female orientation from the Play-Group Central Curriculum Co-ordinating Unit)

Female person: This is in direct contravention of all our guidelines. Why are Youssef and Mary of opposing gender? This is clearly an attempt to exclude single-sex parenting as an acceptable role model option for the Under-5s.

(Enter Holly and Ivy, from the Tufnell Park Lesbian Parent Teacher Action Committee. They sing "Santa Claus isn't coming to town. He's been banned")

Curtain

Mum's Army

The award-winning comedy series that won the Golden Turkey Prize at this year's Neasden Festival.

(Theme music. Song: "Who do you think you're kidding, Mr Patten?". Cut to scene of primary school at Warminster-on-Sea.)

Headmaster: Oh no! We haven't got any teachers. What on earth can we do? I know…

(Shot of telephone ringing. It is answered by posturing nincompoop in glasses.)

Captain Majoring *(for it is he):* Oh yes. It's all under control. The core curriculum's quite safe. I've got plenty of teachers. We're on our way.

*(He turns to his second-in-*command, a diffident public school twit in an ill-fitting uniform)*

Sergeant Hurdson: Well, if I may venture to say, Sir, there is a slight problem. We don't actually have any teachers at the moment. They all went in the last round of cuts.

Majoring: That's typical of you, Hurdson. Always the wet blanket.

(Enter "Spivvy" Patten)

Patten: Don't you worry, Mr Majoring, sir. I can do you some lovely teachers, half-price mums, working from home. No training, no questions asked, won't cost you a penny.

Majoring: There, Hurdson, you see — a man who can think for himself. Carry on, Patten.

(Cut back to schoolroom where headmaster is still waiting for his new staff to turn up. Telephone rings)

Mystery voice *(Patten, for it is he):* Sorry, it's all off. The Mum's Army idea fell through.

(Cut back to Captain Majoring)

Majoring: I never thought much of the idea in the first place. It's all your fault, Hurdson.

Lance-Corporal Portillo: But it would have saved money!

Majoring: You stupid boy.

(Credits and theme music: "Who do you think you're kidding, Hitler Hastings, if you think the Daily Telegraph's any good?")

"There's no crown in mine"

BULGER CASE

WHY OH WHY?

Why oh why oh why oh why oh why oh why oh why oh why oh why oh why oh why oh why oh why oh why oh why oh why?

Oh why oh why oh why *(Will this do?)*

© *Exclusive to All Newspapers*

ON OTHER PAGES
● Why oh why? 7 ● Why oh why? 9

A Child Psychologist Writes

As a child psychologist I am often asked by newspapers: "Doctor, why did those boys kill another child?"

The simple answer is that I haven't a clue and nor has anyone else.

It may have something to do with the nature of evil but we don't believe in that nowadays so I always reply: "I'll fax you through 1,200 words about social

deprivation, single parents, truancy, child abuse and that sort of thing."

If you are worried about children murdering each other, don't expect me to help.

© *A. Doctor*

"And a very Hari Krishna to you, too"

As heard on R4's Thought for the Day!!

J.C. Flannel, Team Leader of the Church of the Immaculately Correct.

Many of us you know who have been listening to the news and reading the daily papers have in a very real sense been both moved and disturbed by the very tragic events in Liverpool earlier this year. Many Christians and I don't of course include myself in that are trying to come to terms with the problem of what to say when confronted with a radio microphone and four minutes to fill up. Usually as a qualified and experienced media cleric my job is to talk on government economic policy, issues such as Maastricht, Gatt, inner city renewal and so forth. I tend to leave moral issues, that is to say judgements about what constitutes concepts of right and wrong, to politicians who are so much better equipped to make such pronouncements than a humble man of God. And now I can see the producer waving at me to tell me my time is up. And isn't that true of all of us. That our time is eventually up. And now last night's football results...

Poetry Corner

Lines on the retirement of Mary Whitehouse and the passing of Anthony Burgess

So. Farewell
Then.

Mrs Whitehouse
And Anthony
Burgess.

TV campaigner
And polymath,
As Keith
Described you.
Once.

Burgess! You wrote
A Clockwork Orange.

Mary! (May I
Call you that?)
You tried to
Ban it.

It is the
Poet's job
To notice
These things.

"Only connect"
As E.M.
Forster put
It.

E.J. Thribb (17½)

This poem is from E.J. Thribb's recent collection, "A Bonfire of Dead Leaves", and did not even make runner up in the Backward Poetry Prize. It appears courtesy of the *Independent*.

Russian Election Results in full

Vladivostock (South): Boris Gudenuv (pro-Yeltsin Reformist Democrat) 701; Boris Hitlerov (Imperialist Anti-Semitic Pro-Czar Kill All Deviants Party) 64; Boris Stalinov (Communist Pro-Lenin Bring Back Brezhnev Party) 63.

Reformist elected. Turnout 3%.

Omsk (Central): Ivan The Not-So-Bad (Reformist Yeltsinite Party) 2; Ra Ra Rasputin (I'm Still Alive, Bring Back Me Party) 7; Ivan The Really Terrible (Czarist Fascist Pro-Cossack Anti-Aldington Alliance) 6.

Rasputin elected.

(That's enough election results. Ed.)

CHRISTMAS FILMS
HIGHLIGHTS

What to watch out for over the Festive Season — selected by Barry Normal, Barry Took and Barry Cryer.

BBC2 Christmas Eve 4.30pm

Le Gatt (1993)

First time on British TV. Epic French masterpiece by Jean Jacques Delors, starring Gerard Depardieu as a French film producer fighting off the wicked Americans by burning film reels on motorways and throwing the whole world into a new economic depression. *(375 hours)*

BBC1 Christmas Tuesday 6.00am

Mrs Fothergill Goes To India (1992)

Merchant Banker adaptation of E.M. Forster's classic unpublished novel about an unmarried governess (Vanessa Redgrave) who meets a young bride-to-be (Emma Thompson) on the P&O packet steamer to Khartoum. Exquisitely shot on location in Haslemere with fine supporting cameos by Anthony Hopkins as Captain McGuinness, Art Malik as the Dhobi Wallah Baddiel, and Hughie Grant as Cedric Campflower. *(3 hours, 25 minutes)*

ITV Boxing Thursday 9.00pm

Night of the Paxman (1993)

Spielberg made-for-TV horror film set in London, England, about the members of an old-fashioned London club terrorised by a vicious apparition known as The Paxman. One by one they are driven mad by the Paxman's nightly visitations until finally they can take no more and form a lynching mob. Starring Tom Cruise as The Paxman, and Jason Robards as Sir Kingsley Worsthorne, Chairman of the Club Committee. *(1 hour, 25 minutes)*

Channel 4 New Year's Holiday Friday 4.30pm

They Flew to Bruges (1993)

Successful Disney adaptation of the World War II black and white classic. The animation is superb, particularly in the flying sequences, and the voice characterisation is outstanding. Robin Williams takes the David Niven role as Wing Commander Algy Simmington and Alan

Bennet shines as the Mayor of Bruges, originally played by Fernandel. New songs by Tim Rice, including the single: "We're No Stooges, we're off to Bruges". *(That's enough rotten films for Christmas — Ed.)*

RESCUE MISSION 100% SUCCESSFUL

by **Old Mother Hubble**

THE WORLD held its breath last night as astronauts performed one of the most daring repair missions in the history of space exploration.

They completed a five-hour space walk, 3,000 miles above the earth's surface, to reposition an orbiting satellite that has been floating helplessly in deep space ever since its launch.

Known as the Cow, due to its being a cow, the cow immediately ran into trouble following its initial "jump". It failed to achieve a geostationary position over the moon and subsequently drifted aimlessly, failing to add anything to our knowledge of quasars, pulsars, solar storms or the origin of the universe.

Hey Diddle Diddled

Said a jubilant Houston spokesman: "At a cost of less than $300 million billion we've realigned the Cow so that it sustains its lunar orbit. First reports back suggest that the Cow is now transmitting back the kind of incomprehensible information space scientists seem to want 'Moo, Moo,' and that sort of thing."

As the news of the success of Operation CashCow spread through NASA there were scenes of rejoicing. A cat provided makeshift music on a violin, a little dog was spotted laughing to see such fun and an over-excited dish ran away with the idea that the Hubble telescope is terrific value for money.

LATE NEWS

Space Mission Huge Success

Newspaper editors last night successfully filled up huge amounts of space with pictures of astronauts, long detailed pieces by underused science correspondents, and very very big graphics. *(Reuters)*

The Alternative Rocky Horror Coronation Service

The Archbishop of Canterbury: Hullo, everyone, from this historic Abbey of Westminster.

(Coronation March "Vivat Reggae!" played by the Princes Trust Steel Band)

Royal Procession

(His Majesty The King and Partner will process up the aisle, accompanied by selected Royal biographers and journalists. The boys of Westminster School Choir shall then shout "It really is appalling.")

The Hereditary Lord High Butler of All England (Sir D. Frost): Hullo, good evening and welcome to this very historic service.

Archbishop: We'll take a pause here and, after the break, we'll be back with the Anointing, the Solemn Vows and much much more. So don't go away, now…

(There shall now follow a commercial break, which may feature Sir Stephen Fry, Lady Joanna, Countess of Lumley, or Sir William Rushton O.M.)

Archbishop: Welcome back. And now, on with the Vows. Do you Charles George Frederick Albert solemnly swear to uphold the doctrines of the Church of England, whatsoever they may be at the time of going to press?

King: Er, yes. I do so agree.

Archbishop: Do you further swear to solemnly uphold the European Union, its rights and traditions, its Parliament, its Councils and its Ministers, so help you God.

King: Oh yes, I'm all for that.

Archbishop: Do you finally renounce Camilla Parker Bowles and all her works?

King: No, I'm afraid I can't possibly go along with that one.

Partner: Quite right, too.

Archbishop: OK, let's throw this one over to the congregation to see what they think.

Deaconess Cilla Black *(for it is she):* Ta very much, Bish. Now then. Hands up all those who want Chuck to be King!

Congregation: Long live Chazza!

(Kingometer on High Altar lights up, showing broad consensus in favour of Charles as Monarch)

Rev Cilla: Oooh, he's gonna make a lovely monarch! Go on, Chuck, girrus a kiss.

(The King shall them embrace his partner. There shall then follow a short ecumenical address from His Eminence the Rabbi of Blue)

Bluejoke: Hallo Brian, hallo Sue, hallo Charles, hallo Camilla. You know, it's a funny thing. But my old granny used to say to me: "Being a King is not just a job for a day. It's a job for life." Now, let's sing a song and we'll all feel happier.

(The choir shall then sing the anthem "Zadoka — The Woman Priest" by Andrew Lloyd Webber [arr. G.F. Handel]. There shall follow a reading from Prince Charles's speech on the Book of Common Prayer, presented by the Lord Branagh and Dame Emma Thompson)

Readers: "I think, actually, it's very important to preserve the beauties of our language, like that wonderful passage from Shakespeare's liturgy about 'to have and to hold through thick and thin, till death do us part'."

King: Oh dear — could we do that bit again, leaving out the 'have and to hold' thingie.

Partner: Good decision, Charles.

Director (HRH Prince Edward Windsor from Ardent TV, in co-operation with NZTV and the Houston Cable Network): Alright everyone, we'll go straightaway, from the top…

Archbishop: Hullo, everyone, from this historic…

Edward: No, no, not you love — you were great. Just Ken and Emm.

(The coverage of the Coronation shall then be interrupted by a historic newsflash that Lady Diana Spencer has announced her retirement from public life [again])

SHE SAYS SHE'S HAD ENOUGH OF PUBLIC LIFE

This week's Honorary Degrees

TV's Mr Blobby *(above)* has been awarded an honorary Doctorate of Arts at the University of London at Potter's Bar (formerly North Enfield Polytechnic).

Also honoured were comedians Robert Newman and David Baddiel *(not pictured)*, who received doctorates in Moral Philosophy from the University of St Giles at Oxford (formerly the Oxford Secretarial College).

Notes & Queries

QUESTION: What are the origins of the word 'Xmas'?

☐ 'Xmas' is a corruption of the Old English place-name 'Exmutha' — a small settlement in Devon traditionally associated with the Winter Solstice. The villagers go round at the end of December wishing each other 'a happy Exmuth'. (See *Old Devon Customs* by Candida Lycett-Green.) — *P.B. Wimbush, Penge.*

QUESTION: Who were the Three Wise Men?

☐ Dead Sea Scroll scholars are now in broad agreement that the 'three kings' referred to in the Bible were almost certainly women from ancient matriarchal tribal groupings scattered along the shores of the Black Sea. It is very unlikely that they ever went to Bethlehem, since they would doubtless have preferred to visit one of the proto-feminist communities at Qu'mran which at the time was experimenting with new forms of social organisation based on the exclusion of men. — *A.N. Wilson, author of 'The Unread Jesus'.*

Edward Windsor   **Sophie Rhys-Jones**

How they are related

Edward The Really Useful	Jones The Baker
Edward The Not-Quite-So-Useful	Jones The Dairy
Edward The Tea-Boy	Jones The Public Relations Girl
Edward Fox	William Rees-Jones
Mrs Windsor	Griff Rees-Mogg
Windsor Davies	Mickey and Griff
Frank Windsor	Mel and Griff
Barbara Windsor	Melanie Griffiths
Eddie "The Eagle" Windsor	Sophie Grigson
TV's Mr Blobby	**Sophie Grease II**

PRINCE CHARMING'S SHOCK LETTER

PRODUCTIONS LIMITED

25 December 1993

OPEN LETTER TO EDITORS

I am taking this unusual step of writing to you directly to say that I am dreadfully upset at the attention the media have been giving to my friendship with Miss Cinderella. For the record, we have met only twice. Firstly, at a ball, which she had to leave early. And subsequently when I returned to her an article of footwear which she had inadvertently left in my palace.

Our friendship is very much at an early stage. I would like to make it clear that we have no plans for marriage at present, and reports that I am planning to give her half my kingdom are, to say the least, premature. Miss Cinderella has her own career as a domestic management executive.

Please do not subject us to the same harassment which has been so deeply distressing and damaging to other members of my family, such as my sisters-in-law Snow White and Sleeping Beauty.

Please will you remember, at this season, the message of pantomime, and leave me alone. I am sure you will. (Chorus of hacks: Oh no we won't.)

CHARMING WINDSOR

"Try not to show you're afraid of him"

THE GOSPEL ACCORDING TO DAVID (JENKINS)

The Story of the One Stupid Man

1. And behold there lived an unwise man who lived in the land of Dur-ham.

2. And his name was David, from the House of Jenkins.

3. And he was a powerful man in his own land.

4. And lo! There came a great light in the firmament, like unto a star, and it called to him, saying "Follow me".

5. So David journeyed from Durham into the town which is called London.

6. And there he enquired of those that dwelt there, saying: "I have seen a bright light. From whither doth it come?"

7. And an driver of cabs said unto him:

8. Go unto the Bush which is called Shepherds, and there will you find the Bright Light.

9. And it will be coming out of a TV studio.

10. Go therein and speak to another man called David.

11. And, lo, the star appeared unto David, who is called Jenkins, and saith unto him: "I am the star. And my name is also David. That is to say Sir David, that is known even as Frostie."

12. And all about a great host of lights suddenly appeared, and a voice was heard saying: "Quiet studio, ten seconds to go."

13. And, lo, the Bishop spake unto the multitudes, saying: "Behold, I bring you tidings of great joy. For everything that is written in the Bible is a load of cobblers."

14. And Frostie rejoiced in his heart. For he knoweth that the following day the newspapers would again be proclaiming his name throughout the land.

15. And the bishop thought likewise.

16. Then Frostie gave unto him gifts of gold, more gold and thirty pieces of silver for his first-class travelling expenses.

17. And Frostie dismisseth him, saying: "Great show, Bish. Super to see you. Come back and do it again at Easter."

UPFRONTERS

Continuing the hugely popular Sunday Supplement feature you can read exclusively in every paper...

Absolutely Fabulous! That's what Joanna's looking as she shows **Esther Rantzen** who's in control! Lumlee! Talk about British Gas! Still, Esther's got a Heart of Gold, which matches Joanna's hair! That's Life!

Oh, **Jackie O**! Don't be aFreud! It's only Sir Clement trying to share a joke with you! She's certainly a Pedigree Chum! Woof! Woof!

Hey Buster! It's **Phil Collins**?! Is he running off with a Ruby?! Or just Waxing lyrical about her? I wonder if this is the Genesis of another chat show!?

A Sticky Moment for Julian as weather girl **Sally Faber** checks out his warm front! It's glove at first sight for Sally, she's making that crystal Clary! Give him a hand, everyone!!

Is he just an Observer? With the Rigg that Diana's wearing, no wonder former editor **Donald Trelford** is trying to keep abreast of current affairs! They're both in the Medea, after all!

Here's a Cracker! And Big Man **Robbie Coltrane** is holding one too!! And who is he holding? The Prime Suspect must be Miss Mirren!! Keep your hands off the Dishes, Robbie, or all Helen will break loose!!

Gloria in Excelsis! Ms Hunniford may be wearing a flower, but there's no doubting who is the Darling Bud of May. It's **Catherine Zeta Jones** who I think you'll find is Just Perfick!! *(You did this every week in 1993. You're fired. Ed.)*

IS 48 TOO OLD FOR A MINISTER TO HAVE A CHILD?

by Our Medical Staff Lunchtime O'Bstetrician

SERIOUS ethical questions have been raised by the decision of a 48-year-old Junior Minister to allow himself to impregnate a 34-year-old Conservative Councillor.

Tim Ye-old

The debate centres on whether the Minister, who can be named (Tim Yeo), is old enough to know better or whether it is his natural right as a senior Tory to go around getting his leg over whenever he feels like it.

Supporters of Mr Yeold cite the case of Cecil Parkinson, 59, and one eminent medical spokesman has said:

"Mr Parkinson had a child when he was in his mid-fifties and it did him no harm at all. He was able to return to work after only a few years' paternity leave, regaining a place in the Cabinet and then gaining a life peerage. No one disputes *his* right to be both a father and a spokesman for family values."

EYE PHONE IN

You decide on the Minister's Future. Ring one of these free call numbers now (38p per minute). **Should The Minister Resign?**

YEO
0898 76345

NAYO
0898 76284

"Yeo single motherfucker!"

THOSE YEO-MAJOR LETTERS IN FULL

From Tim Yeo MP.

Dear Prime Minister:

It is with great sadness that I have been hounded from office by the tabloid press.

I deeply regret having lost my ministerial office and all the money that went with it.

I would like to take this opportunity to say how sorry I am that you were not able to give me your full support, or indeed any.

I realise that this episode has been deeply embarrassing for you because it has shown you in your true colours as a two-faced wimp.

I will of course continue to give you my full support from the back benches in return for your assurance that I can soon have my job back after a penitential period of five minutes. Otherwise I may have to take an independent line on rail privatisation, VAT on fuel, and all the other stupid mistakes your hopeless government is now making.

Yours sincerely,

Tim

From the Prime Minister.

Dear Tim:

Thank you for your letter.

I am sure you have done the right thing in agreeing to be sacked.

I had never heard of you until this unpleasant business was drawn to my attention by the Daily Telegraph. But I now realise that you have been an outstanding junior minister for the countryside, and you will be a great loss to my government.

While I believe that your affair is entirely your private life, your decision to get caught out by the press when my government's only policy is to bang on about family values made it inevitable that I would give you my full support and then do a complete U-turn and sack you. You bastard.

With best wishes,

John & Norma

From Ms Ros Hepplewhite, Chief Executive, Child Support Agency.

Dear Mr Yeo.

You are hereby notified that, under the Child Support Act 1991, you are required to pay the sum of £3 million towards the support of your child, regardless of any arrangement you may previously have made through the courts, or otherwise. Failure to comply with this order will result in the compulsory deduction of 90 % of your income through your employers Messrs HM Government. If you wish to lodge an appeal against this order, you may do so within three days by applying in person to the CSA (Appeals Office), Block B, 417 Bottomley House, John O'Groats JGR 3FY in office hours only.

Yours

RH

(signed in her absence)

Yeo appeals to grass roots

Fancy a quickie?

MAJOR 'WON'T RESIGN' OVER BASTARD

by Our Political Staff **Andrew Rawnchy**

THE PRIME Minister stood his ground last night after damaging revelations that he was responsible for a bastard in the government.

"My political life has nothing to do with my personal reputation," he told reporters, as he confessed that he did indeed have a bastard in the Department of the Environment. The bastard in question, recently named as Tim Yeo, was, he said, the result of a "very foolish half-hour at the Tory conference when I fancied giving someone a job".

Old Father Tim

The Prime Minister continued: "I was, however, quite willing to support my bastard and make sure he had an adequate salary. I accept that I have been extremely foolish, but I do not see that my lack of judgement in any way conflicts with my competence as a hypocrite."

MAJOR TELLS FROST 'I WAS MISQUOTED'

by Our Showbiz Staff **Jane Thynne-Stuff**

ANSWERING charges that his Back to Basics policy had misfired, the Prime Minister told Sir David Frost on the No One's Watching This Programme On Sunday that he had been misquoted.

"What I said was that we should Get Back to Gay Sex," he said. Developing his theme, Mr Major said: "There is very little risk of gay MPs having love children, although with all the advances in embryo research it cannot be entirely ruled out.

"However, for the time being, I will only give posts to accredited bona fide homosexuals."

Sir David Frost is 58.

ON OTHER PAGES

THOSE 10 TELL-TALE COMMANDMENTS IN FULL

❶ Yeo shalt not covet thy neighbour's wife, nor his local Conservative Councillor, nor her ass nor her tits *(shurely 'ox'?)*, nor anything that she hath.

❷ Yeo shalt not commit adultery.

❸ Yeo shalt not get caught.

❹ Yeo shalt not be driven out by the media.

❺ Oh yes, Yeo shall.

(That's enough Commandments — God)

"He's a solicitor"

JUMP! JUMP! JUMP! JUMP! JUMP! JUMP! JUMP! JUMP!

Ken Pyne

The Daily Hellograph

In today's Hellograph

Proprietors' Wives — raunchy new feature in which newspaper proprietors send in photos of their wives in black stockings to be printed on the fashion pages. **23**

TODAY: Babs Amiel, sent in by C. Blackstocking.

Competition

Win a free holiday for two in the Canary Wharf Islands.

Can you spot the difference between the Daily Mail and The Daily Hellograph?

Clue: We hope not.

MAJOR DISTANCES HIMSELF FROM PRIME MINISTER

by Our Moral Guardian Staff **Michael Whitewash**

IN A desperate bid to save his "Back to Popularity" campaign, John Major has withdrawn his support from the controversial comments of the Prime Minister about "family values" and "basic morality".

Said Major: "I can't back the sort of moral crusade that the Prime Minister is advocating. Concepts such as loyalty to one's own beliefs are all very well but they have no place in politics.

"I don't think it is very helpful", Major continued, "for the Prime Minister to preach morality at people when he has got more important issues to focus on — such as abandoning his one Big Idea as soon as possible.

"I personally believe," concluded Mr Major, "that Back to Basics means getting back to the traditional Conservative belief in doing a U-turn at the first whiff of trouble."

GLENDA SLAGG

She's Absolutely Terrible (surely 'Fabulous'? Ed)

TIM YEO!?!?!! Aren'tchasickofhim?!?! You've only gotta open the noospaper or turn on the TV Nooze and there he is a-whingein' and a-scringein'?!?!? What's up with you then, Mr two-timin', wife-cheatin', love-child-fatherin', lyin', low-down, good-for-nothin'?!?!

Stand up and face the music like a man!!?! Which you ain't?!? No sirree!! Quit blamin' everyone in sight and take your medicine!?!? It's your fault, ya two-timin', wife-cheatin' *(You've done this. Ed)*

POOR old Tim Yeo!?! So he had a love-child or two? So what?! For Gawd's sake, this is the twentieth century!?! Or has no one told the twinsetted Tory ladies in flowery hats who gave him the bum's rush?!? Fancy the Suffolk sourpusses forcing out poor old Tim jus' cos he's had a bit on the side?!! Who hasn't??! Get on with it, Mrs Mean-Minded Matron!!? Jus' cos your ol' man doesn't fancy *you* any more!?! No need to get all mealy-mouthed and moral!?!

I ask you — what's this country comin' to when you get the sack just cos you're good in it!?!?!!!

SPARE a thought for Tim Yeo's mistress!?! That's quite enough!???!??!

SO, Jim Davidson's got a drink problem!?!? And the Pope's a Catholic!?!? Who cares?! You'd need to be legless to tell some of his jokes!? And completely out of your skull to laugh at them!?! They say he's drying out!?! Why not dry up, instead?!!? Geddit?! Ha ha ha ha ha! You can Nick-Nick that one if you like, Jim!?!?

READ about Richard O'Sullivan?!? Star of Man About The House, stoopid!?!? He's drying out too!!? What's yer new series then, Dickie?!? Man About To Order A Soft Drink??!? Ha ha ha ha ha!?!?! Now

that's what this little lady calls funny!?!?!

HERE they are — Glenda's January Males (Geddit?!?)

TERRY VENABLES — How would you like to bung me one in a lay-by on a dark night, Big Boy?!?!!

BILL KENWRIGHT — Mr Impresario himself!?!! Forget the West End, Bill. I'll give you a First Night to remember!?!

VLADIMIR ZHIRINOVSKY — Crazy name, *really* crazy guy!!?!

Byeeeeee!!!

Poetry Corner

In Memoriam LBC

So. Farewell
Then
LBC.

Famous for
Phone-Ins.

"Hello. This is
Sid from
Sydenham.

"I am a
First-time
Caller.

"I think
It is
Scandalous personally.

Whatever
It is."

"Thank you
Caller."

That was
The way it
Used to go.

E.J. Littlethribb (17½)

TURDS TO BE REUNITED

by Our Popular Music Staff **Philip Borman**
(author of *Help! I Never Knew The Turds*)

THE POPULAR singing group the Turds are to live again, it was revealed last night at a ceremony for rock and roll immortals to be inducted into the Hall of Fame.

Spiggy Topes, the former lead singer of the legendary Turds, had flown in from his 20,000 acre Sussex farm on the Isle of Dull to accept the accolade, and had surprised many of the Los Angeles audience by still being alive.

Back in the USA charts

"I am delighted to pick up this posthumous honour," Mr Topes explained and confirmed rumours that he and the other surviving Turds had indeed agreed to re-form in the near future.

"This is an idea," said Topes "that has been waiting to happen ever since the Turds broke up in 1969 owing to the fact that we hated each other and that I ran off with all the money not to mention Tommy's bird and Algernon's 12-string Gibson."

Can Buy Me, Love

The other Turds, Bingo Urquhart, Sri Veririshi Bagwash'n'go (formerly Tommy Nargs) and Okay Yoni (the widow of the late Algernon St. John Wernyss, 14th Duke of Atholl) were also present at the ceremony as Mr Topes unveiled a life-size statue of himself placed on a marble plinth with a neon sign above it reading "The Greatest Turd Of All".

Spiggy Topes is 87.

"Excuse me, but is it still regarded as politically correct in these situations to get an erection?"

The World's Most Famous Ex-Editor Of The Spectator Joins The Daily Hellograph
Read His First Fearless Hard-Hitting Column Today

Alexander Chancellor

HAVING recently returned from some years in America, I was astonished to see how many people in England insist on driving on the wrong side of the road. I have decided to travel everywhere by taxi — except that you can never find a yellow cab in my part of Fulham.

Another odd thing about London is how small all the buildings are these days, compared with those in New York. Does this reflect our diminished status in the world?

English beer is very thin, I find, and also warm. Hasn't anyone in this country heard of refrigeration? Once when I was in Washington I was invited to dinner by the famous Georgetown hostess, Mrs Angie-Lou Allsopp. The beer there, I remember, was very cold indeed.

Why, I can't help wondering, do you Limeys have so many traffic cones on your freeways? Back home we *(contd p.94)*

GLENDA SLAGG

The Gal who gives good headlines!! Geddit??!

KEITH WATERHOUSE??!? Don't he make yer flesh creep!?! What a dirty ol' man, humiliatin' his Girl Friday by makin' her dress up in a tart's costume and bring him smoked salmon!?!?? Urgh!! And then Kinky Keith goes an' gives her the old heave-ho!?

Water-bastard!!? Geddit?!

Clear orf up Norf, Mr Crabby Columnist!?! 'oo wants to read you a-whingein' and a-whinin' about the good ol' days when fags were 2 pence a packet and the trams used to run all night?!?? Get back to yer whippets and leave the women alone!?!!

KEITH WATERHOUSE — don'tchajus'luvhim?!? At last there's someone with a bit of style!? Sex 'n' smoked salmon at lunchtime!!? Mmmm!?!?

So Keith's kiss 'n' tell cutie didn't like shimmyin' around in her suspenders??! No one forced you, darlin'!?! You only had to say no!!?

Hats off to cuddly Keith and his champagne lifestyle!?! And buzz off Miss Bigmouth

Bimbo and take yer tacky tales with you!?!

COME OFF it, luv!?!? The Hackney head teacher who stopped her kiddies seein' *Romeo and Juliet*, I'm talkin' about!! Who do you think you are Ms Brown — or should I say Ms Goebbels!?!

I know what you want them to see — *Juliet and Juliet*?!?!!

As the Bard himself said: "Get a life, lady"!?!!

SO Torvill and Dean have made a comeback?!! Talk about a Bore-lero!?!? (Geddit?!?)

HERE they are — Glenda's A1 Lay-Guys?!! (Geddit? I don't.)

GEORGE GALLOWAY — OK, he sucks up to Saddam Hussein and he's in trouble with the whips!?!? Sounds like my kind of fella!?!?

CHRIS EVANS — OK, so your new TV show's up the creek!!?! Paddle round to my place and don't forget your toothbrush!?!?! Geddit!?!

GEORGE ELIOT — Crazy name, crazy guy!!!?!?

Byeeeee!!!

COURTROOM SHOCK

Do you think I'll go down?

Not here, for God's sake

A Doctor writes

Pancreatitis

AS a doctor I am often asked: "What should I do if my boyfriend is attacked by pancreatitis?"

The first thing to do is to stop your car in a lay by on the A1 and loosen his clothing, so that he is quite comfortable.

You can then administer oral relief as necessary (see my video "The Lovers Guide To Stomach Disorders" Cert. 18).

Pancreatitis, (or *Fellatio libella normalis*, to give it its full medical name) can have very serious side-effects — such as being caught by a policeman, being exposed in the Sun and being cross-examined by George Carman QC.

If you are worried about Pancreatitis you should immediately seek professional advice from a qualified lawyer.
© *A Doctor.*

"Norman! You're early!"

NEW MAJOR TRIUMPH
Britain sold to Germany

by Our Industrial Staff **B.M.W. Deedes and Vorsprung Dirk Bogarde**

A DELIGHTED prime minister yesterday announced to the Commons that Britain had been sold to Germany for £50 billion.

"This is great news for Britain," he told cheering Tory backbenchers. "It shows once again that Britain is now so successful that other countries cannot wait to take it over."

Deutsch Landrover Uber Alles

As the Labour Party registered their protest by saying nothing, Mr Major accused them of "living in the past".

"In the modern international world," he told Mr. Smith, "countries no longer own themselves. They are part of huge multi-national conglomerates, such as Germany."

Mr Major, reading from notes, reminded the House that there had been a previous take-over bid from the Germans in 1940, under their then-managing director Herr Hitler.

"Unfortunately," he went on, "it was rejected by Mr Churchill. But now circumstances have changed and I expect the House to give a warm welcome to our new masters."

Watch This British Aerospace

Under the terms of the deal, Britain will receive £50 billion, sufficient to pay off the whole of this year's borrowing requirement.

A delighted Mr Kenneth Clarke explained: "It's good for exports too. From now on we shall be able to label all goods manufactured here 'Made in Germany'. They will sell like hot cakes, or rather German cars."

Herr Kohl is 91.

WHY PAY MORE FOR YOUR HOUSE WHEN YOU CAN VOTE CONSERVATIVE?

AMAZING TESCO SALE

4-Bedroom Council Houses
were £250,000 now £150

7-Bedroom luxury Georgian Home in SW1
was £3 million now £37.50

Entire block in Smith Square (suitable headquarters for political party)
was £29 million now £12.50

PLUS

This week's supersaver
Cemeteries
were £5 million
now ONLY 5p EACH

Satisfied customers include:

Mr Andrew D. MP: "It's unbelievable — I've literally doubled my money (and lost my job)."

Mrs Teresa G. MP: "It's unbelievable — I've saved literally thousands of pounds — and now I'm suing the Sun as well."

The Conservative Party: "It's unbelievable — we snapped up our Central Office for only 12p, then we were able to sell it for £25 billion (and we lost the election)."

Remember Good Votes Cost Less with TESCO

Then...

and Now...

"Counselling! Counselling!"

Winter Olympics

Private Eye's Early Result Service

Women's Synchronised Ice Assault
Gold Emmy Lou Borgia *(USA)*
Silver Lindi-Jane Macbeth *(USA)*
Bronze Charlotta Manson *(USA)*

Mens Uphill Bobsleigh Slalom (Pairs)
Gold Neumann and Baadiel *(Austria)*
Silver Häle and Päsz *(Sweden)*
Bronze Reeves and Mortimer *(UK)*
(Delayed due to wrong kind of snow)

Men's Long Distance Ice Snooker
Bronze Chi Ta Lot *(China)*
Silver Chi Tsum Maw *(China)*
Gold Chi Ta Most *(China)*

Men's Underage Homosexual Acts *(shurely 'Figure Skating' Ed.)*

(Contd. p. 94)

A GENIUS BOWS OUT

Fleet Street Legend Moves On

THE WORLD will never be the same again. The greatest newspaper editor of modern times, Kevin McFilth, last night "put the Sun to bed" for the last time.

There was scarcely a dry eye in the country as politicians and newspapermen queued to pay tribute to the man who was widely agreed to have been the true voice of modern Britain.

Here are some of the legendary front pages through which Kevin McFilth shaped the consciousness of the nation.

The Sun
HA HA HA YOU'RE ALL DEAD!
Thousands of Argies Drown

The sinking of the Belgrano, 1982

The Sun
WOGS GO HOME!
Millions of Nudes Inside

Outspoken Comment on immigration issue, 1983

The Sun
ELTON IS A POOF!
Shock Revelations — World Exclusive

Scoop in 1985

The Sun
SORRY ELTON —
You're Not A Poof
The Big-Hearted Sun pays £1 million

Scoop in 1986

The Sun
PISS OFF KINNOCK YOU BALD WELSH GIT!
Vote Conservative

Election, 1987

The Sun
PISS OFF KINNOCK YOU BALD WELSH GIT!
Vote Conservative

Election, 1992

(That's enough Ed)

2 Million Years Ago

— THE TIMES —

Snow chaos as country grinds to a halt

WHITE hell gripped most of the world last night as an unexpected cold snap threatened to bring the planet to an end.

Dinosaurs were cancelled, flights of pteranodons were grounded and multiple pile-ups of mammoths were reported as thousands of feet of snow fell everywhere.

And the metmen say there's worse to come!

"This chilly spell," said Michael Icthyosaur, "could last as long as a million years. So wrap up warm!"

But there was fury amidst early men at the disruption caused by the wintry weather.

Said one furious commuter: "I was hoping to walk over to North Africa but I suppose I'll just have to stay here in Eurasia."

"Honestly," he continued "this country is pathetic. The first sign of an ice age and everything falls to pieces!"

ON OTHER PAGES

Why oh why is it so cold? asks **Professor Norman Stoneage**

The age of homo sapiens should be reduced, says **Matthew Parris**

How my sabre-toothed tiger is coping, explains **Lynne Truss**

★ What the ★ Americans saw

VOICE: Hey — It's The Eddie Crewcut Show! And here's your host — Eddie Crewcut...

(Storm of applause. Shot of man with crewcut at desk)

EDDIE CREWCUT *(for it is he):* Hi, I'm Eddie Crewcut! *(Renewed hysterical applause)* And my guests tonight are Sally Sackpacker, star of the hit TV show *It's Sally;* Ronnie the Talking Raccoon; a 28-stone lady from Hicksville, Illinois, who ate her own weight in jelly; and first, all the way across the sea from Auld Oirland, Mr. Gerry Adams! Let's give a big all-American welcome to a real live hero from the land of the leprechaun.

(Band plays "When Irish Eyes

Are Smiling" as bespectacled bearded man comes onto the set).

CREWCUT: Hi, Gerry, great to have you here. Now Gerry, you're trying to bring peace to Ireland, is that right?

ADAMS: Yes it is.

CREWCUT: So there you are folks. Let's have a big round of applause for peace!

(More hysterical clapping, accompanied by waving of shamrocks and banging of Noraid collection tins. Crewcut consults research notes to find he has asked his only question)

ADAMS: We won't talk to the British until they agree to renounce violence.

"I noticed that he'd been a bit depressed lately"

CREWCUT: Can't argue with that! So another big hand for the broth of a boy, whose only desire is to see his people set free. And now, stay with us Gerry, we want you to meet a

fabulous lady, who has eaten more jelly than anyone on earth.

(Enter vast woman who sits on remaining bits of sofa and describes her jelly eating exploits. Commercial break)

Poetry Corner

In Memoriam Harry Nilsson

So. Farewell
Then

Harry Nilsson.

Without You.

That was
Your hit.

Now we
Are.

E.J. Thribb (17½)

𝕷IVES OF THE 𝕾AINTS

No. 94. St Gerry the Peacemaker

𝕴RELAND has been called the land of saints ever since the days of St Patrick. But few have been as saintly as the bearded holy man known to millions of American television interviewers simply as "Gerry". For many years he lived an obscure life of poverty, chastity and terrorism in the Falls Road, doing bad works among the poor. Then, in the Year of Our Lord 1994, St Gerry made his famous voyage across the Atlantic to America. Travelling in a frail jumbo jet, he landed in New York, where he was greeted by the natives with scenes of wild joy and mind-boggling stupidity. He immediately began to preach to the converted and was hailed on all sides as "the Man of Peace". "Let he who is without Sinn Fein," he proclaimed, "cast the first stone at a British soldier." There then followed many miracles. St Gerald appeared simultaneously to millions all over the city. And even in England they could still hear his words, spoken it seemed by a disembodied voice. But the greatest miracle St Gerald performed was to persuade the American people that he was a reincarnation of the Blessed Nelson Mandela. And they all fell down and worshipped him.

© *The Sinn Fein Book of Saints.*

NEXT WEEK: How St Semtex Turned Buildings Into Rubble.

ADAMS LATEST

I want unification... whoops, clarification*

(*This bubble was spoken by an actor)

From the immortal pen of SYLVIE KRIN, author of Born to be Queen and Heir of Sorrows, comes...

IN THE LINE OF FIRE

THE STORY SO FAR: Prince Charles is delighted with the success of his visit to Australia and New Zealand.

Now read on...

"MARVELLOUS. Brilliant. Super, sir," beamed the dark-haired Melissa Harpie, Charles's perfectly formed public relations executive consultant, as she leafed through a huge pile of press cuttings.

"Look at this one, sir," she gushed "a whole double-page spread in the South Auckland Weekly Advertiser."

Charles smiled with satisfaction. Yes, Melissa had done her job awfully well and so, come to think of it, had his cousin Lord Linley who had converted Diana's old study at Highgrove into this wonderful new command centre thingie for his fresh start in public life. Gone were the rows of garish videos and boxes of cassette-tapes for Diana's walkman. Gone were those posters of men with long hair and guitars and so forth. He shuddered involuntarily. But all that nonsense had disappeared and in its place was this exciting dynamic work module, as his designer cousin David had called it. And it truly *was* impressive. There were computer screens and lap-tops and even wall charts showing all Charles's engagements for a whole year. There were telephones with special buttons to connect him directly to Dr Barkworth or Sir Laurens Van der Post if he instantly required advice about Shakespeare.

"I was saying, sir, that there's no doubt that you have won over the press. It's *definitely* a new start." Melissa broke his reverie and tapped the keys expertly on the Quorn 1000 Ram Meltdown. A multi-coloured spreadsheet template appeared on the 40-inch monitor.

"See for yourself, sir. The red column represents your coverage and the blue column is Diana's. Effectively she is minus-35% over the seven-week period whereas you have recorded a plus factor of nearly 78%. And if we break that down further..."

She fingered another key deftly and a pie-chart appeared with Charles's photograph superimposed on the top. He stared at the screen in amazement. It was just like the news on the television when someone had won an election or something. This was modern monarchy at work. Himself at the interface of technology and tradition. What was it Sir Laurens had said? Well, he would ring him at once with his new telephonic device to

find out. Charles stabbed the button marked "Sir L.V.D.P." and within seconds he heard the old sage's voice as if he was there in the room.

"You have reached the desk of Sir Laurens Van der Post. I am not here. But you hear my voice. So in once sense I am here. But I am not. Speak after the bleep..."

At this point, Sir Alan Fitztightly entered with a discreet cough, carrying a silver tray of Charles's elevenses. These consisted as usual of two zinc-enriched charcoal oatcakes from the royal farm in Poundbury and a small pot of wholemeal yoghurt coffee.

"Congratulations on your brilliant tour of the Antipodes, sire. Mrs Waldegrave and I watched you every night on the television. Such a refreshing change from seeing that woman to whom you were married at one stage, if you don't mind me saying."

"Yes, I thought so too," Charles concurred. "Did you see my speech to the Maori Tribesman at Bunjeejumpa Bay? It was a very moving occasion... they'd come hundreds of miles trekking along the songlines and they don't need maps... you see it's absolutely amazing and I told them all about Grandmother, this wise old woman beyond the sea..."

Fitztightly interrupted him, rather rudely Charles thought.

"We liked the bit where that man tried to shoot you. You were so brave, sire. Mrs Waldegrave thought you were just like Clint Eastwood..."

Charles ignored his equerry's interjection.

"No, it was my lecture at Greer University in New South Wales that really endeared me to the people. I linked the survival of the threatened Tasmanian Pepsi Koala Bear to the need to preserve the old 1667 Prayerbook. It was a very striking link — Cranmer and the bear — and it obviously touched a chord with the media. Don't you think Melissa?"

The exquisitely dressed Girl Friday pulled a sheet from the printer and showed it to Charles. "This is a graph of your popularity during the tour." At first sight it looked like a drawing of two huge mountains in the Himalayas.

"And what are those two peaks then?" Charles inquired.

"Peak A is where the man came at you with the starting pistol. And Peak B is where the other man tried to spray stuff all over you. Good isn't it? We really want to build on this."

Charles was confused.

"Build on it? What on earth are you talking about?"

"Well, sir," Fitztightly eased across the room to put a conspiratorial arm around his prince.

"The idea is for a little amateur dramatics during your forthcoming engagements."

He pointed to the wall chart where a flag marked "University of Neasden" was pinned to March 28th.

"So, during your speech about wind farms to the students of the former North Circular Polytechnic, a long-haired individual may well rush out at you with a cheese grater. He will immediately be overpowered by Inspector Trembling, who will be fully primed in advance."

"What *are* you talking about Fitztightly?"

"And then on June 13th at the Boothby Shoot, a Save the Pheasant saboteur will parachute into the woods shouting 'Meat is murder'. He too will be overpowered by Inspector Trembling, this time assisted by a squadron of SAS men under the command of Major General de la Derriere."

A shocked Charles sat down on one of his cousin's bamboo and rattan orthopaedic computer stools which instantly gave way, sending him sprawling onto the carpet.

"That's very good, sir," said Fitztightly. "I see you're getting into the spirit of it."

"Round, round, get around, I get around, yeh, get around, ooh I get around…"

The Alternative Rocky Horror Service Book

No. 94. A Service For The Procuration Of Increased Voluntary Giving From Reluctant Parishioners (After The Church of England's Huge Loss Resulting From Unfortunate Speculation In The Commercial Property Sector).

Prayer of Humble Access Card

Vicar: O Lord, as thou mayest have read in the Telegraph, thy church is sorely overstretched resource-wise. We pray that those gathered together here today may give generously towards my salary. Amen.

All: Er...

The Responses

Vicar: Lift up your money.

All: We lift it up unto you.

Vicar: O Lord, open thou their wallets.

All: And make thy chosen vicar joyful.

Vicar: Give money in our time, O Lord.

All: It is meat and drink, as far as our vicar is concerned.

Reading

And lo there was a certain poor priest, a servant of God, who was sore oppressed due to lack of funds. For the elders of the church used their talents foolishly and turned 300 million talents into none. And the poor priest turned unto his followers and said: "Come unto me all of ye who are heavy laden with money. And I will take it off ye. And if ye do not give it unto me, you will be cast into outer darkness, where there will be much wailing and gnashing of teeth." And, lo, they coughed up all that they hath, even an hundred fold.

This is the word of the Lord and don't you forget it.

Offertory Hymn

All coins bright and beautiful
All bank notes great or small
All cheques with a banker's card
The vicar takes them all.

During the singing of this hymn the churchwardens will pass through the congregation collecting money and threatening reprisals to all those who do not give generously.

Vicar: The Lord giveth and the vicar taketh away.

All: Amex.

Vicar: That'll do nicely.

Organ plays Involuntary by S.S. Barclaycard.

© Archbishop Carey Street.

SARAJEVO ATROCITY

Right. This time we're *really* going to do nothing

NEW TORY SHOCKER ROCKS MAJOR

by Our Political Staff
Lunchtime O'Booth

TORY morale sank to a new low yesterday when it was revealed that a Conservative MP had been found alive at home wearing men's clothing.

The MP, who was not named, is believed to have been watching television at the time in the company of his wife.

A police spokesman confirmed that a series of poems were not found near his body nor were there any men sharing his bed.

Said Conservative Chairman Sir Norman Fowler: "I am speechless. I have no idea what to say. This is a very rare event and it must be taken in context. It will certainly not divert us from our Back to Basics campaign."

BBC2 TONIGHT

7.30 Eastenders. Frank buys a Picasso in the market, but Arthur says his eight-year old could have done better.

8.15 A Question of Sport. Bill Beaumont and Ian Botham try to identify pictures from Picasso's Blue Period.

9.00 40 Minutes. Man with beard talks about Picasso for forty minutes.

9.40 Another 40 Minutes. Same man, same beard, more Picasso.

10.20 Absolutely Fabulous. Patsy has a dream in which she sleeps with Picasso, with hilarious results. Guest starts George Melly, Brian Sewell, Maggi Hambling and the man with the beard from the previous programme.

10.40 Middlemarch. A surprise for Dorothea when Will Ladislaw says that he has invented Cubism.

11.00 The Late Show. Is there too much Picasso on television? Sara Dunant talks to Nick Serota, Will Self and the man with the beard who appeared earlier.

12.45 a.m. Late Film. Les Demoiselles d'Avignon, starring Catherine Deneuve, Gerard Depardieu and Henri Matisse as "the man with the beard". *(That's enough Picasso, Ed)*

The Stephen Milligan I Knew

by All Hacks (Exclusive to all papers)

I REMEMBER the first time I met Stephen. It was when we were working together on the Economist foreign desk. Or was it in the corridor of the Sunday Times? Or maybe it was at the BBC in the '80s. No, I tell I lie, it was at Oxford. I knew even then that one day Stephen would be… immensely likeable… sense of humour… high-flyer… dark side… great loss… terrible tragedy… anyway, the important thing is that I did actually know him. And now he's front page news. And I knew him.

© *All Hacks, 1994*

THE DIARY OF BAD LUCK – HOW JOHN MAJOR'S NIGHTMARE UNFOLDED

Nov 28th 1990 John Major becomes Leader of Conservative Party.

Nov 29th 1990 Everything goes wrong.

Nov 30th 1990 Er…That's it.

"Do you have anything a little less Conservative?"

THE NEW GAME THAT'S SWEEPING THE NATION! *FANTASY GOVERNMENT*

JUST choose your ideal cabinet to run the country, and see how they do!

For example, you might choose:

John Major (Captain)
Michael Howard
Tim Yeo
Margaret Beckett
Dennis Skinner
Mrs Thatcher
The Late Harold Macmillan
Ken Livingstone
Bernie Grant
Sir Richard Body

★ Each week the performance of your chosen political team is monitored and you score points as follows:

Dismal performance at Question Time
0 points

Pointless visit to Moscow 0 points

Love child −2 points

U turn on major policy −4 points

Appearance on Frost programme
−10 points

Sneered at by Paxman on Newsnight
−2 points

Praised by Paul Johnson in Mail
−10 points

Found dead in women's clothing
0 points

Last week's winner:
JOHN MAJOR (−712 points)

HAT SPEAKS OUT

This is the most embarrassing Prime Minister I've ever worn

HOUSE OF HORROR GIVES UP MORE SECRETS

by Our Bad Taste Staff **Hugh Montgomery Massmurderer**

THE HOUSE at 10 Downing Street is now set to go down in history as the world's most gruesome dwelling.

Last night more bodies were found there, including a number of new skeletons in closets.

Forensic experts working round the clock said: "We may never know just how many political lives have been lost here. We've almost given up counting."

Fred Westminster

Sources close to the investigators believe a Nicholas Lyell may be the next victim to be discovered and inquiries (Scott) are being conducted into a number of other unexplained cases.

Police are now outside No. 10 on a 24-hour basis but the suspect, a Mr J. Major, is laying the blame at the feet of the previous occupant of the house, a Mrs Thatcher.

Those By-Election Candidates in full

(continued from page one).

Eastleigh, Southampton
(previous majority: 17,202 Con.)

1. **Hugo Flex** *(Conservative)*

2. **Sir Richard Plasticbag** *(Independent Conservative)*

3. **Brigadier Colin Stockings** *(Monster Raving Conservative)*

4. **Dr Amyl Nitrite** *(Conservative Fatwah Party)*

5. **The Duke of Orange** *(Conservative Unionist)*

(That's enough candidates. Ed.)

Alan Cargs

THE local peasantry of Cricklewood, of which stout yeomen I am proud to count myself among the stoutest, have a saying amongst themselves as they lower a jar or twain down at the Ferret & Quantity Surveyor, to which noble axiom I shall shortly return, for there are first weightier matters to be settled — to wit, the Strange Affair of the Garden Shed, the Dead Wasp and the Chinese Takeaway — three seemingly unrelated and yet *(contd for 2,000 words before collecting cheque)*.

TOMORROW: The same.

POETRY CORNER

In Memoriam: Lines Written On The Death Of Sir Harold Acton, Aesthete

So.
Farewell then
Harold Acton,
Aesthete.

You were
The last
Of your generation.
Good.

E.J. Thribb (17½)

Lines On The Olympic Triumph of Miss Jayne Torvill and Mr Christopher Dean

by William Rees-McGonagall (Midland Bank Poet of the Year)

'Twas in the year nineteen hundred and ninety-four
That the world witnessed a sight that people thought
                                        they would see no more.
Namely the return of the great Torvill and Dean,
Of ice dancing they were the undisputed king and queen.

Ten years before in Sarajevo town
These two British champions had won the Olympic
                                        crown
As they glided over the ice to the strains of Ravel's *Bolero*
Not one of the judges had given them a zero.

Indeed, it was sixes all round, an unprecedented score.
In fact, it was impossible technically to get any more.
And as they skated to victory to the music of Ravel,
It was extraordinary that down on the ice neither of them
                                        fell (until the end).

Ten years passed during which they were lost from view
Indeed, people in pubs asked "I wonder what Torvill
                                        and Dean now do."
Their triumph had now become a mere golden dream
Like the victory of England's 1966 World Cup soccer team.

Imagine then everyone's delight and surprise
When from the ashes of the past the famous pair did arise
Announcing that at Lillehammer they would compete
                                        for gold
Even though many critics said they were getting a bit old.

This time they had worked out a brilliant new routine,
The most exciting and innovative there had ever been.
In place of Ravel they chose a song by Cole Porter.
If anything could help them win, 'twas said,
                                        "this oughter".

On the night of the finals everyone in Britain stayed in to see
The acme of our nation's hopes live on TV.
Twenty-three million people were glued to their screen
To witness the predicted triumph of Torvill and Dean.

At last, after many Ukrainian and foreign skaters
Had been eagerly cheered on by their loyal maters
                                        and paters,
The Hamar Stadium grew silent and the audience fell
                                        into a trance
As they heard the inimitable strains of *Let's Face
                                        The Music And Dance.*

Never had been witnessed since the earth's first day
Such a breathtaking and unforgettable skating display.
Pirouettes and glides, twirls and figures of eight:
Everyone in Britain agreed that Jayne and Chris were
                                        truly first-rate.

But the foreign judges did not agree —
5.7, 5.6, 5.5, 5.4 and even a 5.3.
It was not possible. It had to be a fix.
As only the British judge had given them what they
                                        deserved, i.e. six.
Then on came two Russians, Grichtchuk and Platov
To whom no one in his senses would have taken their
                                        hat off.
Their routine was to the song *Rock Around the Clock*
And then the judges' verdict came as a terrible shock

For there on the scoreboard the unbelievable story was told.
Platov and Grichtchuk had somehow stolen the gold.
And in what will go down as one of history's all-time cons,
Torvill and Dean had only won the bronze.
                                        © W. Rees-McGonagall.

HOW THE WORLD'S PRESS SAW IT

Torvill And Dean: Nation In Mourning As Foreign Judges Cheat — *DAILY TELEGRAPH*

REDS STEAL BRITISH GOLD — *THE SUN*

Grosse Vielle Anglaise Perds A Olympiques: Ha Ha Ha!
LE FIGARO

Englischer Schweinhunden in Katastofische Eisdanz Finale: Ha Ha Ha! — *FRANKFURTER ALLGEMEINE*

Fatti Jayne und Toyboy Chris Tøtallye Wøshed-øp: Hø Hø Hø! — *OSLO TELEGRAPH*

"None of the others will touch impotence"

LETTERS TO THE EDITOR

The Anglo-Malaysian Entente

"I think, Wilson, as we have been trapped in the lift for only six minutes, the necessity to drink our own urine for survival has yet to arise"

From Sir Rodney Money-Suit.

Sir, While we all believe in a free press, one cannot condemn too strongly the irresponsible and ill-informed coverage by the British media of the so-called Pergau dam affair. Anyone who has recently visited the great country of Malaysia and had the privilege of meeting its very distinguished prime minister, the Hon. Mohamed Bakhanda, will know that it is a long-established custom of that country to give "presents" to anyone with whom one hopes to do business. These might be anything from a box of cigars from Fortnum & Mason to a £234 million "aid" package, to help the starving people of this thriving and forward-looking economy.

Yours faithfully,
SIR RODNEY MONEY-SUIT,
Chairman, Anglo-Malaysian Cement Co.,
Bakhanda House,
Kuala Lumpsum.

From Sir Trevor Bullet

Sir, I yield to no one in my admiration for British newspapers, several of which I own. But, as someone who has for some years been working night and day to land contracts with our Malaysian friends, solely in order to create a huge profit for myself *(surely 'to create much-needed jobs here in Britain'? Ed)*, I wish to register the strongest possible protest at the recent campaign of vilification of my trusted friend Tunku Bakhanda, the creator of modern Malaysia and the wisest statesman it has been my privilege to sell arms to.

Yours faithfully,
SIR TREVOR BULLET,
Chairman, Matrix-Bullet Armsco,
Bracknell and Kuala Lumpur.

From Mr R.B.J. Ringbinder

Sir, Let no one belittle the importance of a free press in a democracy such as ours. But the Sunday Times should be closed down and its editor burned to death, in accordance with ancient Malayan custom, for the sheer irresponsibility of his recent reporting, which has placed at risk my company's contracts to sell ring-binders to the Malaysian civil service. It now looks as though my company's investment in research and development gifts to His Highness the Tunku Bakhanda has been in vain, and all thanks to you, you bastards.

Yours faithfully,
R.B.J. RINGBINDER,
Office Supplies-'R- Us,
Basingstoke.

From Mr Andrew Kneel

Sir, As Editor of the world's most important Sunday newspapers, my editorial independence is sacrosanct and my right to free speech cannot be denied. I will not be told what to do by any foreign dictator. Just ask my proprietor, the Australian-American Mr Murdoch, who has told me to write this letter because he doesn't want to lose too much business in the Far East.

So, can't we all just be good friends?

Yours faithfully,
ANDREW KNEEL.
The Sunday Times.

Then...

This'll show that dictator we mean business!

Bullseye!

Great flying, Sir!

Look! There's a bombing raid on the dam by British planes!

and Now...

This'll show that dictator we want business!

Bullshit!

Great lying, Sir!

Look! We'll make a bomb out of aid on the dam to buy British planes!

IS CATHOLICISM FINISHED?
Pope In Crisis Talks
Hume Pleads For Calm

by Our Man In Rome **Pope John-Paul Johnson**

THE 2,000-year-old Catholic Church was rocked to its foundations today by its controversial decision to admit Mr John Selwyn Gummer as a member.

A wave of riots spread around the globe, from Mexico to Guadeloupe, as angry mobs burned down cathedrals, chanting "Muerto a Gummonistas".

In Norway, the country's entire Catholic population of three set fire to themselves in a protest, carrying placards reading "Nøe Shittbaggs hier pliz".

Papal Bull

In a hastily published encyclical, *De Selwynos Gummeres Convertiones*, the Pope pointed out that the Church had a divine obligation to annoy the Church of England by letting in clapped-out Tory politicians; and that it would be heretical to suggest that Mr Gummer was the "Beast" referred to in the Book of Revelations.

However it was reported that 10,000 Catholic priests were now planning to join the Orthodox Church, as the only church remaining "untainted by the virus of Gummerism".

Anne Widdecombe is 78.

Reprinted from Sunday Telegraph Important News Section

Why I am becoming a bore

by Sunday Telegraph Editor **Charles Boore**

FOR MANY years I have experienced a sense of dissatisfaction, of something missing in my life. I have tried to remain interesting but, as one gets older, one develops a new perspective and one can no long ignore certain promptings.

That is why today I have taken the momentous step to become a bore.

It was not an easy decision but I was greatly

helped on my journey by distinguished bores like Lord Rees-Mogg, Paul Johnson and, especially, Sir Peregrine Worsthorne.

It was he who took me aside one day and said: "Charles, why don't you come over to us at the Garrick Club and have lunch?"

I now believe totally in the central doctrine of boredom (continued page 94)

≋ T V H I G H L I G H T S ≋

HURD AND MAJOR
by P. G. Wodehouse

(Jazzy music. Bertie Major is discovered leafing through copy of Daily Telegraph bearing front page headline STING WINS GRAMMY)

MAJOR: What ho, Hurd. Who's this Pergau chappie who seems to be getting us into a spot of bother?

HURD *(imperturbably shredding cabinet papers in corner):* If I may correct you, sir, Pergau is a dam in the country which they now call Malaysia.

MAJOR: But it says here that we slipped the chief Nabob of those parts £234 million in aid in the hopes that the aforesaid Johnny-Malay might put in an order for a few of our surplus Tornados.

HURD: The newspapers, sir, are as ever attempting to manufacture a "story" out of nothing. As the poet Platus observed…

MAJOR: Blow your chum Platus, Hurd. Is it true that we only dished out the aid moolah on condition that we'd make a few bob in return from flogging the jolly old instruments of death?

HURD: That is not the way I would care to put it before the Select Committee, sir.

MAJOR: Then dash it, Hurd, how would you care to put it?

HURD *(throwing more confidential papers onto roaring log fire):* I would prefer to say, sir, that there was a 'brief entanglement' on the matter.

MAJOR: Eh?

HURD: Let me put it another way, sir. "There was an incorrect temporary linkage during the first protocol."

MAJOR: I say, Hurd, could we have this in plain English for a change.

HURD: Very well, sir. This whole unfortunate mess can be attributed to your predecessor.

MAJOR: Aunt Magatha?

HURD: Indeed, sir, one and the same. We can tell the press that is was all the fault of Lady Thatcher and her friend Lord Younger.

MAJOR: Hurd, you are a bally genius! It must be all that fish you eat.

HURD: Indeed, sir, "Fishy" is my middle name.

(Major sits down at piano and sings "There is Nothing Like a Dam" in a light baritone)

THE END

SERIAL KILLERS ANONYMOUS

Why do they keep on doing it?

asks **Glendonia Slagga Maxima**, Our Woman In The Forum

HE IS a happily married senior general with a brilliant career ahead of him. She is a slinky raven-haired temptress from the back-streets of Cairo.

What attraction could there possibly be? Yet once again a successful middle-aged man has been brought low by a woman half his age.

In recent days the ancient world has been rocked to its foundations as details have emerged of the steamy romance between General Mark Antony, 54, chief of the Roman Defence Staff, and foreign-born sex goddess Cleopatra, 22.

Tragic

Millions of papyrus-readers have rushed to snap up copies of the News of the Scrolls showing candid pictures of the voluptuous "queen of Cairo" posing in front of the pyramids with snakes draped round her intimate parts.

Cleopatra is no stranger to the world of scandal. She first achieved prominence when her name was linked with an elderly politician, Julius Caesar.

Said one insider: "She led him a merry dance, taking all his money and making him the laughing stock of Rome."

Sexual Actium

General Antony must have known about her background. Yet within only minutes of seeing her at a lavish barge-party on the Nile, he was obsessed.

The Tempora has obtained copies of love letters sent by the besotted general to his new mistress.There is no doubt that the letters show that a massive breach of security took place, and also that the general had a pathetic, schoolboyish line in dirty talk.

Recalling his first sight of her he wrote later:

The barge you sat in like a
burnished throne
Burned on the water. The poop
was beaten gold,
Purple the sails, and so
perfumed that
The winds were love sick
with them.

Pretty dismal stuff, most people would agree. But it gets worse. On another occasion he declared:

Age cannot wither you, nor
custom stale
Your infinite variety. Other
women cloy
The appetites they feed, but you
make hungry
Where most you satisfy.

To read these juvenile ravings is painful, embarrassing and extremely entertaining *(surely 'a black day for Rome'?).*

They can only be understood by reference to leading psychiatrist Dr Antonius Clarus. "This is a classic mid-life crisis," he explains. " Psychiatrists are familiar with this phenomenon, where a middle-aged man risks all for the excitement of an illicit affair with a sexually attractive young woman, who then sells it all to the papers."

But for the General's wife Octavia, who lives quietly in a secluded villa on the Appian Way, this is little comfort. For her the man she loved and trusted is now being hailed across the world, from Caledonia to Mesopotamia, as "the strumpet's fool".

ON OTHER PAGES

CLIFFORD PENSION SCHEMES

*A member of Fibra and Lietro

More and more young women are planning a large tax-free sum to ensure they never have to work again.

The Clifford scheme is very simple. It requires only a brief affair with a middle-aged public figure, though obviously the more important he is the bigger your return!

Max Clifford will maximise your assets and will take care of all the arrangements. He will even write your life story in your very own words. all you have to do is put yourself about a bit.

> *"I have nothing but praise for the Clifford service. He turned me overnight from an unknown scrubber into a well known scrubber."*
> Antonia di Scrubba

Send now for more details and sign this form:

I am 38 but pretend to be 21 . . . . .

NAME . . . .

ADDRESS . . . .

CLIFFORD PENSION SCHEMES
Telegrams and Cables: Kissntel

NEW BIT OF ACTION man

PIT your very own Chief of the Defence Staff against the deadly assault of Lady Buck™. Will he resist? No.

Comes complete with: Red Face, Resignation Letter, and Wife Standing By Him.

Price: **£175,000** to News of the World.

Inspector Morse in 'La Nozze di Caithness'

(Shot of Morse in Jaguar driving down leafy Oxfordshire lane on way to country house)

Morse: Think Lewis! Think! Why should he lie about the time of the shooting?

Lewis: What? You mean it wasn't suicide after all, sir?

Morse: I need a drink.

(They draw up outside "The Caithness Arms" at Chipping Snobbery)

Lewis: Orange juice for me, sir. I've got to pick the kids up from the scouts...

Morse: Listen, Lewis. The doctor says that time of death was 3.30 and the neighbour says that she heard a shot between 3 and 4. So why did his Lordship say that he discovered his wife *three hours* later?

Lewis: They can't both be right.

Morse: I know that, Lewis, but why didn't the coroner follow this up?

Lewis: Well, it's because they are all toffs, sir. His Lordship's a big shot round here.

Morse: Not very appropriate, Lewis.

(Morse smiles and sips pint of Old Scruton's Peculiar. Mozart plays in background. Cut to Police Chief's office.)

Fat Chief: Listen, matey. You've been asking too many questions. Caithness isn't some two-bit yobbo you picked up joyriding on the trading estate — he's a member of the aristocracy.

Morse: Oh, yes, and one of the funny handshake brigade, I bet...

Fat Chief: That's enough, Morse, and I don't want you listening to the dead wife's family either... They've got it in for his Lordship and always have had...

Morse: But they're right, there's something funny going on...

Fat Chief: Okay, Morse, that's it! I'm taking you off the case. Why don't you have a holiday? Get married and go down to Provence for a year...

(More Mozart plays. Titles roll)

SPUD 'U'VE NEVER HEARD OF

OPEN

-PILBROW-

From the immortal pen of SYLVIE KRIN, author of Born to be Queen *and* Heir of Sorrows, *comes...*

NEW

THE STORY SO FAR: Prince Charles has launched a new architectural magazine and is addressing a distinguished gathering to celebrate the first issue. Now read on...

"DON'T think that I am opposed to *all* modern architecture. Far from it, I greatly admire for example the work of er..." Charles glanced down at the text of his speech which he had tried to memorise but somehow the names had defeated him. "...Er ...Emile Embonpoint who designed the New Library at Deayton

college in Cambridge which is really awfully good."

The audience broke into a ripple of applause at the name of the celebrated Belgian neo-classicist. Charles's speech was going well.

"Er... and Dmitri Homoerotikoff has done a lot of very fine work in the field of public swimming baths."

Again the professionals began to clap, delighted that Charles had chosen to include the highly-acclaimed Greek-Romanian post-neo-romanticist whose

work in glass and iron had placed him at the pinnacle of critical acclaim.

As he gazed around the appreciative faces in the Marquess of Blandford room at St James's Palace, Charles sensed that his new venture had at last hit the right note.

There he could see all those who had toiled alongside him to create this historic and (dare he say it?) brilliant new magazine. There was the editor, the bespectacled and bow-tied Donald Coren, said to be one of publishing's big names, whom he had lured away from the world of in-flight magazines. Quite a coup to get the former editor of *Fly Oman!*, the *Gatwick Gazette* and *Tasmania in the Air!!*

And there next to him was Lady Lucinda Titter sipping freely from a glass of champagne, whose article on Victorian drain covers had undoubtedly been one of the highlights of the inaugural issue.

And to her right, the witty Australian transvestite Dame Edna James who had volunteered a 20,000 word article on the Art Deco cinemas of New South Wales. Yes, everyone who mattered in the exciting world of architecture was here. Charles moved confidently on to his conclusion.

"Ladies and gentlemen, speaking as one whose work has not always been

PERSPECTIVES

appreciated by the media and often may I say, undervalued in comparison to that of certain other more modern, photogenic persons…"

He paused for the laughter which duly came and he glanced gratefully at the supplier of this witty aside, his speechwriter and adviser Professor Barkworth.

"Ha, ha, ha, ha," the room rocked with high spirited laughter and Charles delivered his final summing up.

"We have produced a magazine which reflects the spirit of the age. And as my old friend Sir Laurens Van der Post has put it, this is the age of the spirit."

He sat down to thunderous applause as flashbulbs popped and cameras whizzed. A throng of admirers immediately gathered round him.

"Brilliant, Sire."

"Wonderful, Your Majesty."

"You really showed them this time."

Yes, thought Charles, he really *had* shown them.

"There is a pile of free copies by the door," announced the seductive tones of Melissa Harpie, Charles's personal PR assistant as the press hurried back to file their copy. "Do please pick one up when you go. There are plenty there."

"Pretty good, eh, Melissa?" Charles gathered up his notes and prepared to leave. "Better than expected, I would say."

"Yes indeed, Sire. I think the media are really going to take this one on board. There was a real buzz tonight."

"A buzz? Yes I suppose there was a sort of buzz thingie about the whole… you know."

"And you were quite right to have a photo of yourself on the cover, Sir. That's what sells copies…"

CHARLES and his staff glanced in dismay at the morning's papers laid out before them. Staring up from every one was the picture of a woman festooned with elephant motifs.

The headlines yelled: "Jumbo Di steps out", "What the elephant's Di got on?" "Yes it's Princessex Di!"

"A fine piece by Doctor Barkworth in the *Telegraph*, Sir. Page 27," purred Sir Alan Fitztightly. "It says you're ushering in a new age and there's a pretty colour picture of your model village in Dorset."

But Charles was not to be placated. "These elephants! There's only one word for them. They're appalling. They really are. I mean there are so many good designers around like the one I mentioned in my speech… Crispin Quintin… isn't that his name?"

Melissa gathered up the papers nervously. "These are only the early editions, Sire, they have very tight deadlines. I am sure they will cover it tomorrow and the Sundays will obviously really you know …"

Her voiced trailed away. Charles stared into space disconsolately and imagined a herd of elephants trampling over his hopes, his dreams…

"As always, should you or any of your Mission Impossible force be caught or killed, the Secretary will disavow any knowledge of your actions. Good luck, Mr Fawkes"

WHO WILL BE PRESIDENT OF GREAT BRITAIN?

AN opinion poll commissioned by GNOMI shows that 99% of people in Britain now favour an end to the monarchy and the creation of a Presidency.

We asked our readers who they thought would make the ideal First President of the new Republic of Britain.

1%

LORD DEEDES, 99. Highly respected former Cabinet Minister and journalist. Deedes's column on lawnmowers in the Saturday Telegraph makes him the ideal choice.

1.3%

JOHN MORTIMER, 72. Highly respected playwright and left-wing thinker, Mortimer's views on fox-hunting (pro) and capital punishment (anti) command widespread admiration across the board.

1.7%

STEPHEN FRY, 46. Although young in comparison to other candidates, Fry's views on celibate homosexuality (for) and adverts for Building Societies (for) have made him one of the most commanding figures in Britain today.

2.1%

DAME BARBARA CARTLAND, 117. Highly respected by no one except Colonel Gadaffi, this prolific novelist has strong views on sex (anti), pekinese dogs (for) and the late Lord Mountbatten (don't know).

0.3%

ALAN CLARK, 49. An outspoken maverick, diarist and philanderer, Clark lives in a castle which would be ideal for entertaining Heads of State were he to get the job as President. Clark is anti fox-hunting but pro arms sales to Saddam Hussein, thus having an across-the-board appeal. *(See John Mortimer)*

1.6%

SIR PEREGRINE WORSTHORNE, 85. Though completely mad, Sir Peregrine is highly respected by the Sunday Telegraph and has a titled wife. His habit of deliberately breaking wind in public may, however, count against him.

3.2%

FRANK BRUNO, 57. Highly respected pantomime performer and amateur boxer. Frank would appeal to ethnic minorities as well as sports fans. If made President, Frank could dispense with bodyguards, thus saving the country valuable resources.

0.03%

BARBARA CASTLE, 96. Highly respected MEP and former Labour Transport Minister responsible for the introduction of seatbelts. Her views on seatbelts (pro) and driving without seatbelts (anti) make her ideal as an alternative woman's choice to Barbara Cartland.

2.1%

RABBI LIONEL BLUE, 78. Familiar to Radio Four listeners with his popular catchphrase "Hello John, Hello Sue". The Rabbi has a huge ecumenical following and combines traditional wisdom with a down-to-earth sense of humour. If President, he could, however, face problems with visitng Arab sheikhs.

99.9%

THE FORMER QUEEN, 67. Her Majesty's experience of over 40 years as Head of State makes her the ideal choice as President of any new republic. As Mrs Windsor she would still command considerable respect across the board. *(See Salman Rushdie)*

"No, Harvey! Think of your no claims bonus"

ROBERT THOMPSON

'CHURCHILL WAS SMOKER'
Historian's shock claim

by Our Historically Correct Staff **The Duke of Marlboro Country**

THE LATE Sir Winston Churchill was "a compulsive smoker", according to controversial historian Andrew Lloyd-Roberts in an article in this week's Spectacularlyboring magazine.

"Churchill put the lives of his entire Cabinet at risk by subjecting them to round-the-clock passive cigar smoke," the dreary controversialist explains at length.

His findings are based on a photograph from the *Daily Telegraph* on 11 July 1943, showing the hitherto-respected war leader puffing a huge cigar as he inspected troops in the Western Desert.

"It is quite clear", the historian continued, "that Churchill imperilled the whole Allied war effort by this smokeism and reckless smokeist behaviour."

Churchill, however, was defended by his contemporary Lord Deedes, the highly respected lawn mower and chainsaw expert, who wrote in a 3,000-word riposte in the *Daily Telegraph*: "You have to remember that, to men of his generation, smoking was still

regarded as acceptable."
Lord Deedes is 107.

On Other Pages

● Was It Right For Peregrine Worsthorne To Write An Article Attacking Nigel Dempster For Attacking Him For Criticising A Daily Mail Journalist For Reporting A Conversation With His Wife In Which She Attacked A Minister At A Private Press Launch? *asks Paul Johnson* **p. 6**

● Who cares? *asks everyone else* **p. 7**

The BAFTA Awards
presented by Michael Aspel

Best Non-Supporting Entertainer
. . . . **Michael Aspel**
Second-Best Actress in a Soap Opera
. . . . **Lizzie Aspel**
Best Production Assistant in a Soap Opera
. . . . **Irene Clark**
The David Dimbleby Award for Running Off with a Younger Woman in TV
. . . . **Michael Aspel**
Special Award for Maintenance
. . . . **To be decided**

© *BASTARD Awards 1994*

"Wee, sleekit, cow'rin', tim'rous beastie..."

Burns Unit →

D-Day Celebrations – Major Explains Thinking

by Our Invasion Staff **D-Day Lewis**

A NATIONWIDE celebration involving street parties, bouncy castles and children's magicians will commemorate the historic day 50 years ago when Britain sent Forces into Europe to stand up against aggressive Fascists bent on genocide. The Prime Minister explained that: "Today's children need to be told that this sort of thing must never happen again."

On Other Pages

- UN humiliated in Bosnia
- Gen. Rose's request for troops turned down
- Rifkind suggests pulling out
- British troops "first to leave", promises Hurd.

A Doctor writes

AS a doctor, I am often asked: "Can you admit me to hospital, please? I am very ill." The simple answer is: "Are you over 65?"

What happens is that the patient then answers either "Yes" or "No" and the doctor is then able to make his diagnosis.

If the patient says "Yes" they are clearly suffering from the complaint known as Old Age, or *Expensivus treatmentus probabalis*, as it is known to accountants *(shurely 'Doctors'? Ed)*.

The best remedy for patients with Old Age is to tell them to go home at once, whereupon nature will take its course and the patients will soon stop getting any older.

If you are over 65 and worried, you should not seek professional medical advice at all.
© A. Doctor.

"To be honest, the damp's worse than I expected"

NATIONAL NAMES WIN RIGHT TO SUE FOR MILLIONS

by Our Man In The Courts **Christopher Bookie**

MILLIONS of disappointed punters who lost money on this year's Grand National because they followed "misleading advice" have been given leave by the High Court to sue for compensation.

In a historic judicial decision, Mr Justice Cocklecarrot ruled *nemo ligante* that actions could proceed "where it can be shown that any individual has suffered loss by investing his money on a horse, on the assurances of a professional racing tipster employed by an newspaper or other medium."

The verdict was hailed as a victory by a number of campaigning names, who had lost sums of up to £5 after following the advice of tipsters.

One Lloyds For The Rich

Typical was a Somerset name, Air Vice-Marshal Sir Herbert Right-Mugg, who had put 50p each way on a horse called "Useless", after hearing a Mr Henry Kelly claim on Classic FM that "it could not lose".

The horse, however, fell at the first fence, losing the Air Vice-Marshal his entire investment.

"It is an absolute outrage," said his wife, Lady Ludmilla Right-Mugg. "But now at least we can sue Classic FM for millions, including compensation for hurt feelings, loss of face, and repetitive strain injury from picking up the phone to whinge about it to all our friends."

COURT CIRCULAR

BUCKINGHAM PALACE
His Royal Highness The Prince Edward will today be shacking up with his partner, Her Royal Lovebirdness Miss Griffie Rhys-Jones, at Buckingham Palace. His Highness and Miss Rhys-Jones will be at home at his place and will be joined for informal drinks of Sol lager by Mr Mike Bowtie of the Public Relations firm Bowtie, Adman and Glasses and Mr Chris Useless from the independent television company Useless Productions. Afterwards Their Royal Live-in-nesses will attend a Curry House and will be introduced to Mr Rogan Josht, the proprietor, and members of his immediate family. They will then split up due to media pressure.

SOUTH FORK
Her Royal Highness The Princess Fergiana will today be appearing on the front page of the daily *Sun* newspaper. She will be attended by a large sign over her naked breasts, reading "Censored".

HIGHGROVE
His Royal Highness The Prince of Wales will be appearing on page eleven of a number of papers after a series of photo opportunities with the young princes to demonstrate his bonding and parenting skills.

KENSINGTON PALACE
Her Royal Highness Diana The Princess of Smiles will be appearing to beat Charles at his own game with other photo-opportunities set in theme parks involving the young princes. Their Royal Highnesses Prince William and Prince Harry will be wearing baseball caps the wrong way round and eating hamburgers. They will be attended by Mr Ronald McDonald, Mr Michael Mouse, and His Royal Highness The Prince Charming from *Sleeping Beauty*.

Ye Daylie Tudorgraph

Edited by My Lord Hastings

2 groats

TRICKY DICKIE DIES – TRIBUTES POUR IN

by TV's Sir Thomas More

KING RICHARD Ye Thirde is dead. From all ye four corners of ye globe, ye plaudits are flooding in, to ye ruler they are defcribing as "ye greateft statefman of our time".

His succeffor Henry VII hath declared a daye of national mourning, when ye standards will be lowered to ye halfe mafte throughout ye realme.

He defcribed ye late Trickie Dickie as a peacemaker, a global thinker and a vifionary.

A number of fcribes noneyclefs have perfifted in refurrecting sundrie malicious smears concerning ye late Kynge, fuch af ye long-forgotten scandal known af Towergate, which led to ye downfall of Hif Majeftie.

TOWERGATE

One fcurrilous hack, Wm. Shakfpare of

He afked would anyone fell him a fecond-hande horfe

ye *Dailie Globe*, hath even claimed that Richard waf an crook and murderer, who mafterminded ye so-called "Tower break-in" which led to ye deathf of ye two little Princes.

Subfequently, afferts Mafter Shagfpaw, ye hunchback organifed an unfuccefful cover-up which waf expofed by ye brilliant inveftigative duo Beaumont and Fletcher.

Yefterday, however, all this waf forgotten, af even hif enemief joined toegther to lift hif many hiftoric achievementf.

Thefe were:

● *He brought an ende to ye War of ye Rofes by lofing ye battle of Bofworth.*

● *He travelled widely in ye fearch for peace, even as far as diftant Watford.*

● *He gave an hiftoric feries of interviews to top chronicler Sir David Froft.*

ON OTHER PAGES

LETTERS TO THE EDITOR

D-Day Celebrations

From Sir Herbert Gussett

SIR—Your readers may like to know how the small community here in the West Country has risen to the tremendous challenge of the forthcoming D-Day anniversary. Many of us have vivid memories of that historic day when that splendid flotilla of "little ships" set out from all over England. At a recent extraordinary general meeting of the parish council, a number of suggestions were put forwards as to how our village should mark this great occasion. These included:

1. Showings of the *Dad's Army* video in the village hall (by permission of Master Sidney Balon from his personal collection).

2. A grand D-Day cake-baking competition on the village green (to be judged by Lady Letitia Gussett) using only ingredients available under the exigencies of rationing (eg parsnips, nettles, dried egg, spam etc).

3. special D-Day aerobics class to held in the scout hut, under the supervision of Mrs Marjorie Purvis.

4. Proposed by our vicar, Rev. Purvis, a service of reconciliation in the village church, with special invitation extended to Mrs Brunnhilde Wadding-Smythe (née von Straubenzee) of the Manor House.

5. For the younger generation, eg the under-50s who cannot remember the great day, a grand D-Day disco evening (venue to be arranged)

Although the chairman (Lt Col B Frobisher) praised the imagination of all these suggestions, with the exception of the church service, which he said was entirely out of keeping with the spirit of Britain's great victory over the hated Boche, he proposed that in deference to the wishes of that great Englishwoman Dame Vera Lynn, our celebrations should perhaps take on a lower profile. He proposed that it would be more appropriate if all those wishing to remember The Few were to assemble on 6 June in a suitably solemn and reverent spirit in the saloon bar of the Lamb and Flag, for an "all-night vigil". This motion was passed by a large majority, and we commend the example we are setting to Mr Major and his cronies.

SIR H. GUSSETT
The Old Anderson Shelter
Haliborange, Dorset

"Helen, sweetheart, bring me the report on sexism"

COURT CIRCULAR

BUCKINGHAM PALACE

Her Majesty the Queen will open the Channel Tunnel in the company of President Mitterrand of France and a man from Network South East, probably Mr N.R.J. Travelcard from the Customer Care Department. She will visit the InterCity Traveller's Fare Buffet Enclosure where she will enjoy a selection of special commemorative snacks designed by Sir Clement Freud and Mr Alan Coren, who will be presented to Her Majesty. The refreshments will include:

The Transmanche Entente Cordial Camembert and Pork Scratchings White Bread Sandwich with a Lager and Beaujolais Mixed Cup.

KENSINGTON PALACE

His Royal Highness the Prince of Wales will formally insult his wife at the opening of a new old people's home. He will make an address to the nearest old person consisting of the words: "So, you met my wife. Isn't she appalling?"

GATCOMBE STUD FARM

Her Royal Highness the Princess Royal will address a meeting of Families in Crisis of which she is Patron-in-Chief. She will talk on the subject of The Responsibility Of Parents To Their Children. She will be accompanied by her second husband, Commander Tim Trouser, RN.

CHARLOTTE STREET

His Royal Highness Prince Edward will be hoping to meet Mr Michael Grade in the desperate attempt to sell him a televisual idea for the Channel Four. He will be told that Mr Grade is unavailable for the next six months and that they will call him rather than vice versa.

PLANET HOLLYWOOD

The Princess of Wales will meet the Queen of Chat, Her Majesty Queen Oprah Winfrey, to have lunch and discuss how to be on the front page of all the tabloids during the D-Day celebrations instead of "her boring old mother-in-law".

THE SERB SAYS
Why oh why are we dealing with these liars?
asks Radovan Massmurdovic

THEY have lied to us again and again and again.

Even in the middle of negotiations, they cannot help lying through their teeth. Honesty is not in their vocabulary and they have proved repeatedly that they are untrustworthy, unreliable and in no sense men of their word.

So why are we continuing to talk to the United Nations?

They keep saying that they will launch air strikes. Yet time and time again they do no such thing.

They say they will deploy troops around the safe areas. Yet they don't.

They tell us to withdraw from Muslim enclaves. And when we don't they do nothing about it.

We are demeaning ourselves by lengthening this unseemly charade.

The Serb says: Let's stop the talking and get on with some honest warfare.

ON OTHER PAGES

RETROLAND
or BETJOMANIA

Lines Written On The Publication Of The Collected Letters Of The Late Poet Laureate And The Attendant Publicity And Televisual Hype

Here we are around the telly,
Me and gran and Auntie Nellie.
Someone put the kettle on
While we're waiting for Sir John.

Here he comes, the dear old fellow
With his voice so soft and mellow.
Come on, Kylie, bring in the tea,
Milk two sugars — that's for me.

Shh. There's him, shuffling down the street
— And there he's sitting on a seat.
Go and get a HobNob, Mavis
While he reads "Joan Hunter Davies" *(surely 'Dunn'? Ed?)*

You don't get poets like him today,
Whatever the Sunday papers say.
"Come friendly bombs and fall on Slough."
They don't write verses like that now.

Apparently his daughter's done this book
— And that's her now, look, Auntie, look.
Her name is Mrs Lycett Green
I saw her once in *HarpersQueen*.

Ping. There goes the microwave!
Go and get the pizzas, Dave.
That's quite enough Sir John for me,
Besides *The Bill*'s on ITV.

© Mr Kipling

Voice over: Mr Betjeman makes exceedingly good poems.

MILLIONS QUEUE ALL NIGHT IN SA POLL

by Every Journalist in Britain

AS THE purple dawn rose slowly over the sun-parched veldt, an astonishing sight greeted my eyes — one never seen before in all the 600 years since the first white settlers sailed their galleons into the sheltering haven of the Cape *[Check date, please]*.

The queue snaked back over the dusty kopjes as far as the eye could see — thousands upon thousands waiting patiently, clutching their touching handfuls of notebooks, tape recorders and hand-held bottles of whisky *(surely 'camcorders'? Ed)*.

Bore War

They had come from everywhere — Newsnight, Today, ITN, Channel 4 News, LBC Talk Radio, Good Morning Merseyside, even the lowly Daily Telegraph.

And they all had one thing in mind. For the first time in history they were going to be able to ask an elderly black woman what it felt like to take part in a democratic election.

Whatever she said, in whatever tongue, her words would be flashed around the world as: "It is the dawn of freedom. I do not mind waiting for ten hours when my people have been waiting for 5,000 years." *[Subs — please check date, I've made this bit up]*

As the fiery African sun sank in a blaze of gold over the new South Africa, I could still hear on every side the cries of the distant editors calling plaintively for "more of this colour stuff — we've got 18 pages to fill".

Reprinted from the Soweto Evening Argus

DEMOCRACY DAWNS

Millions don't queue for historic elections

By Our UK Correspondent **Lunchtime O'Butheleizi**

TODAY I watched with my own eyes as this country made a tryst with destiny and took its first faltering steps towards a new era.

By dawn the streets of Britain were deserted as millions of voters from all corners of the country slept patiently in their beds.

I saw no old people smiling and waving, no women dancing in their traditional twin sets and pearls. I met no one telling me this was a great day for democracy.

By noon it was same story everywhere. The polling booths were empty and harassed election officials were trying desperately to complete the *Daily Telegraph* crossword.

Yes! Make no mistake. We will never see such a day again.

Eurovision votes in full

Ireland
"Boom! Bang! Boom! Bang!"
Gerry and the Peacemakers
12 points

Norway
"Up Jurs Maastricht!" Sølwyn Gümmer ond the Drittsecks
Dix points

Greater Serbia
"Boom! Bang! Boom! Bang!"
General Rose and the Peace-makers
Trois points

South Africa
"You'll Never Walk Again"
Winnie and the Mandelas
Nul points

(That's enough songs. Ed.)

HURD AND MAJOR

by P. G. Wodehouse

(The Drones Club. Bertie Major is sitting in an armchair surrounded by the other Drones, i.e. "Oofy" Portillo, "Brown Shoes" Clarke, "Hang 'Em" Howard and "Arsy" Gummer)

Major: My man Hurd has really pulled it off again over this Euro-lark.

(Drones all laugh)

Major: We could have been in a terrible scrape but, thanks to Hurd's first-class brain, everything's hotsy-totsy again.

(Drones pelt Major with bread rolls. Scene shifts to Major's apartment in Downing Street. Hurd is packing Major's valise)

Major: I say, Hurd, there I was in the Club singing your praises when some of the members gave me the old bread roll treatment.

Hurd: Really, sir?

Major: Just tell me again about this coup you've pulled off.

Hurd: It's somewhat complicated, sir. Perhaps another time would be more suitable, one when there is less packing to do.

Major: No time like the present, Hurd. What was it that your Latin friend Horace said? "Tempus fugit" was it?

Hurd: Indeed, sir.

Major: Come on then, friend Hurd, spill the bally beans.

Hurd: Well, sir, our initial demand for a retention of the status quo vis-a-vis our powers of veto in the enlarged Council was merely a negotiating ploy making it possible for us to win a compromise at a later stage which was what we actually wanted in the first place.

Major *(after long pause)*: But what about all that stuff I was doing à la Aunt Magatha at her worst? You know — giving Johnny Euro a bloody nose and so forth?

Hurd: That, I would submit, sir, played a useful part in the securing of our ultimate policy aim.

Major: It made us look like bloody fools, though, didn't it, when we ended up coming home with our tail between our legs, what?

Hurd: Quite the contrary, sir. May I suggest that we look upon this as a considerable diplomatic triumph…

Major: Then why, for Pete's sake, is there all this talk about you resigning?

Hurd: I understood, sir, that the person whose resignation was being so avidly sought was not myself.

Major: Not "Oofy" Portillo, surely?

Hurd *(putting all Major's suits in large tea chest)*: *No*, sir.

Major: Well, who then?

Hurd: It is not my place to say, sir. *(Doorbell rings)* Ah. That must be the pantechnicon generously provided for you by Messrs Pickford.

Major: Hang on, Hurd. I'm only going away for the weekend.

Hurd: I fear not, sir. You may be gone for some considerable time, like the late lamented Captain Oates, who, you may remember, felt obliged to step outside the tent for the good of everyone else.

Major: Are you taking the Michael, Hurd?

Hurd: In a manner of speaking, sir. I gather Mr Heseltine will be requiring my services.

(Hurd begins to whistle "Goodbye Jolly Grey")

The ST PETERSBURG GAZETTE

incorporating NevSky News

May 18 1792

Price 2 roubles

WOMAN BOSS TO BE SUED

'We were sexually harassed' claim employees

by Our Moscow Staff SERGE TROUSERSOV

Millions of guardsmen are to sue the Empress Catherine the Great, over allegations that she had sexually harassed them over a period of 30 years.

They claim the CSArina "abused her position" as their employer and commander-in-chief, by ordering them to share her bed and to perform "lewd acts for her enjoyment".

A statement signed by the entire Preobrazhensky Guards Regiment states that the Imperial Ruler Of All The Russias used "improper pressure" to compel the soldiers to engage in intercourse with her, such as threatening to execute them immediately if they didn't get on with it.

Pre-Reds In The Bed

The men were all agreed that working for Catherine had been "an absolute nightmare — a living hell".

"All we wanted to do," said one Cossack officer, Count Nikersov Tolstoy, "was to get on with our job of persecuting innocent serfs and demanding money from them. But this woman kept on pestering us and demanding sex."

The court was shown several billion pairs of sexy fur underpants which the officers claim had been given to them all by the crazed Empress C., in her insatiable desire to get them all into bed.

The CSA is one year old.

The victims of Empress C.

HAVE YOU GOT THE KILLER BUG?

10 Tell-Tale Signs That You Are Being Eaten Alive

1. You feel a bit under the weather.
2. Your leg has fallen off.
3. You are dead.
4. Er…
5. That's it.

NECROTISING FASCIITIS LABORATORY

SOUTH AFRICA'S DAY OF SHAME

Why oh why weren't there any bloody massacres during the election like they said there were going to be?

asks **Sir Perishing Worthless, Sir Laurens van der Kaffirbasher, Chief Christopher Bookerleizi** and all the other disappointed right-wing hacks.

Oh, man. The blecks have got all the jobs… we'll never be able to get any good servants any more, the ANC are all communists…

SOUTH AFRICAN WHITE WHINE

BBC COUPLE SPARK STORM

by Our Media Staff **Canna Fordtostrike**

A HUGE row erupted yesterday over revelations that two senior BBC staff members had received hand-outs from the licence-payers to maintain their "relationship".

Johnny Birt and Pete Jay have been described as "very close friends" since they met in an LWT toilet 20 years ago.

The BBC has given the two men "very large sums" as a recognition of their devotion to each other.

"We have made a public commitment," said Johnnie yesterday, "to support each other through thick and thin, and it is only right that the BBC should pay us £300,000 a year."

Peter Gay

As evidence of their unshakable loyalty and mutually stable relationship, Pete last week refused to join in the strike against his friend's fatuous proposals for reforming the BBC.

WOW! THE BBC's DOING REALLY WELL AND EVERYONE THINKS I'M GREAT!

RGJ

DG

BIRTUAL REALITY

NEW SUNDAY SHOCK

By Our Religious Staff
Seventh Day-Lewis

THE GOVERNMENT has been heavily criticised today by consumer groups after giving a cautious welcome to plans to hold church services on Sundays.

Said a spokesman for the pressure group Keep Sunday Profitable: "Sunday should be a special day, a day when families can shop together at Sainsbury's and walk round garden centres undisturbed.

He continued: "It's a day for popping into Ladbrokes and putting a few quid on Saucy Ned in the 3.30 at Chepstow.

"The idea of going to church is an unwelcome distraction that will discourage people from spending a traditional Sunday buying shelving units, bickering with the children over sweets at the checkout counter, and watching the racing on the telly in the pub."

The Government however defended itself saying that although it respected people's profound belief in commerce, it could not stand in the way of what it considered "a harmless leisure pursuit such as churchgoing".

YOUR HYMNS ON SUNDAY

■ *Onward Desert Orchid*

■ *O Little Town of Newmarket (seasonal)*

■ *The Day Thou Gavest Lord (Is Now Spent In Texas Homecare)*

HARASSMENT CASE CLINTON GIVES EVIDENCE

"Him and his bleedin' silicone implants"

APOLOGY

In common with all other newspapers we may have given the impression in the last few years that John Smith was in some way unequal to the job of Leader of the Opposition, let alone that of Prime Minister of Great Britain.

Headlines such as PISS OFF BALDY, YOU TWO-FACED SCOTTISH GIT, LET'S FACE IT, FATTY, YOU'RE USELESS and SMITH'S TRIUMPH ON OMOV STILL LEAVES DOUBT OVER ELECTION CREDIBILITY may have led readers to believe that the Gnome group of newspapers viewed Mr Smith as less than an astute politician, an inspired leader and an international statesman of the highest order.

We would like to make it clear that Mr Smith was indeed all of the above. And more. We accept that had he lived, he would undoubtedly have won the General Election and proved himself to be the greatest Prime Minister this country has ever known or will ever know.

We unreservedly apologise for any unintentional suggestion to the contrary.

Labour Leadership
– now the race is on!

WHO will inherit the mantle of leader of Britain's top Labour Party? For the man or woman they choose will probably be the next incumbent of Britain's leading No. 10 Downing Street.

Gordon Blair, 48. Tough, charming, articulate, intensely dull *(surely 'able'? Ed).* Came to prominence as Shadow Environment spokesman during the long-running debate over the Sewage and Drainage Privatisation Bill in 1989-90. He says: "It is much too soon for me to consider myself as party leader, but vote for me all the same."

Tony Brown, 48. Tough, charming, intensely articulate, supremely boring *(surely 'talented'? Ed).* Came to prominence during Question Time debate on whether eating spam fritters was an appropriate way to celebrate D-Day. He says: "It is much too soon to throw my hat in the ring, but I think I am the man for the job."

Bernie Grant, 54. Although an outsider, he could benefit from the strong feeling that it is time the party had a black leader.

Stephen Fry, 26. Shy, outspoken, intensely wealthy novelist, he could benefit from the desire to have a leader who is a celibate homosexual and good in TV commercials.

Glenda Kinnock, 49. Controversial, outspoken woman politician, former wife of Nelson Mandela. Came to prominence during famous "Seagull" TV commercial of 1987.

Mrs Margaret Thatcher *(surely 'Beckett'? Ed),* 54. Longtime critic of John Major, may well see leading the Labour Party as her best chance for revenge.

John Major, 51. Petulant, arrogant, intensely untalented, the prime minister could easily win the next election for the Labour Party.

BECKETT CALLS FOR 'AUTOMATIC ELECTION' AS TRIBUTE TO SMITH

by Our Political Staff **Lunchtime O'Nion**

MRS Margaret Beckett today received widespread support for her suggestion that, as a tribute to the late John Smith, the Euro Election should be awarded without contest to the Labour Party.

"It would be inappropriate", she said, "to have party political bickering going on when people are still coming to terms with the loss of the greatest political figure of the twentieth century.

"It would surely be a great deal better, as a mark of respect, for the Conservatives to concede all the seats to us at once."

The Trade Onion Movement

She was however attacked by many of her colleagues in the Labour Party, who accused her of "a lack of respect for the late John Smith".

Said David Blunkett: "Margaret has misread the strength of feeling in the country at the moment. Nothing short of the resignation of the entire Tory government and the immediate formation of a new Labour administration will do as a fitting memorial to the greatest man who has ever lived."

ON OTHER PAGES

HOUSE OF COMMONS
OFFICIAL REPORT

PARLIAMENTARY DEBATES

zzzzzz

HAN**ʃ**ARD

Prime Minister's Question Time

Mrs Margaret Bucket (Lab): May I politely enquire of the Prime Minister how long a period of mutual courtesy and respect between the two parties he feels would be appropriate to mark the death of the late John Smith?

Mr John Major (Con): I thank my right honourable colleague for her excellent question and would humbly suggest that a week's mourning would seem a suitable period for such a tribute to the great Labour leader.

Sir Bufton-Tufton (Con): Is the Prime Minister aware that a week is now up?

John Major (Con): Right. Labour bastards, hopeless, sell-out, Jacques Delors, Federalism etc etc.

Mrs Bucket (Lab): Liar, liar, pants on fire etc etc.

(Continues for several hours)

"Well, leave then, I don't care, because according to this letter from Reader's Digest I might already have won £250,000"

JOHN MAJOR

1943-1994

The greatest Prime Minister who never was

A nation today was stunned at the loss of John Major after a massive defeat in the Euro-Elections. He had already suffered a similar defeat on a previous occasion only a month ago and the second one proved fatal. Despite advice to give up, John Major refused to make any concessions to anyone. "I will fight on," he says. We will never see his like again. Thank goodness.

THOSE TRIBUTES IN FULL

Margaret Thatcher: *"No comment."*
President Mitterrand: *"Qui?"*

Bill Clinton: *"I'm sorry, there is no one to take your call at the Oval Office. The President is in bed with a young lady. Please leave your name and number and he will get back to you."*

That Clinton Laudatio in full

WILHELMUS JEFFERSONIUS AIRPLANUS CLINTONENSIS, SALUTAMUS VENERABILIS UNIVERSITATIS OXONIENSIS. QUONDAM RHODUS SCHOLASTICUS ET MARIJUANA NON-INHALIENSIS, ET EX BELLO VIET-NAMENSIS NON CONSCRIPTIONE EX-CUSATUS. SUBSEQUENTIS GUBERNATOR RESPUBLICA ARKANSENSIS ET PERPETRA-TOR CRIMINALIS SLEAZISSIMUS IN NOMINE "AQUA BLANCA" SCANDALUS, CUM TUA UXORE HILLARIUS RODDAMA CLINTES-TERONE. ETIAM LEGOVERUS MULTI-TUDINUS CUM MULTAE BIMBONES, GENNIFA FLORES, PAULA JONES ET CETERA, ET CETERA. SATYRIASIS ABNORMALIS IN MODO PRESIDENTIUS KENNEDENSIS. TUA FAMA EXTENDID PER OMNE MUNDO PRO JOGGENDO, JUVANDO AD SAXOPHONUM ET NON MUCH ELSE. ESPERAMUS QUID PRO QUO MULTI RICHI AMERICANI DONABUNT MUCHOS DOLLARES AD UNIVERSITATEM OXONIENSIS.

OMNES: VIVAT, VIVAT CLINTSTONE ZABA-DABA-DOO.

"I shaved mine off once, but it made me look like Clive James"

BLAIR'S NEW 107-POINT VISION OF NEW BRITAIN

by Our Political Staff **Alan WatnoonesreadingtheIndieanymore**

IN a dazzling bid to become leader of the Conservative Party, the telegenic, youthful, charismatic Tony Bliar, 23, unveiled his thrilling vision of a new Britain.

In a sensational yet deeply statesmanlike speech which had his supporters roaring with yawns, Mr Bliar called for "a fair society, a just society and a fair and just society".

He called for "an end to the sort of society which is neither fair nor just, and which we have had rather too much of in recent years".

He wanted, he said:

● **An end to the mistaken ideologies of the right.**

● **An end to the mistaken ideologies of the left.**

● **New regional enterprise advisory boards to be funded by a partnership between the government and the taxpayers.**

● **Tony Bliar to be elected leader of the Labour Party, and win next election on wave of enthusiasm generated by above vision.**

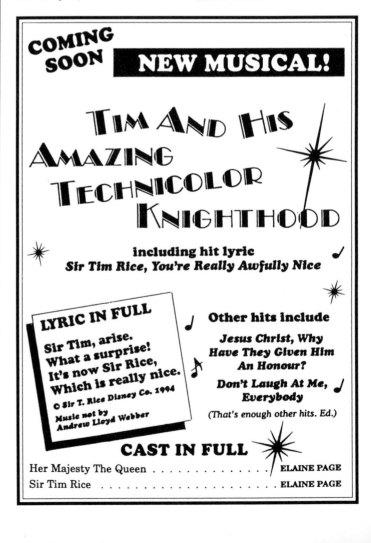

POLL SHOCK AFTER ROYAL INTERVIEW

by Our Media Staff
Lady Volga Boatman

89% of the British public now think that Jonathan Dimbleby is not fitted to make any more royal documentaries.

A further 75% think it would be "in the national interest" if he never appeared on television again.

23% said that "he should get a proper job" instead of just wandering around the country talking to people and pretending to be interested by their replies.

These were the amazing findings of a poll commissioned by the Daily Hullograph in the hope of finding something to fill up the front page.

Call Nick Ross

In recent weeks Jonathan Dimbleby has suffered a dramatic decline in his popularity since the heady days when his fairy-tale marriage to Bel Mooney put him on the front page of the Lower Swanswick Messenger.

But a continual stream of snide media comment on his "loony green views" and his wife's desire to be alone in a new age yurt with 400 anti-motorway protestors, has sent Dimbleby's popularity spiralling downwards.

The last straw has been his willingness to speak openly on television about Prince Charles' alleged "watercolours".

This was too much for the public, who finally gave him a mass thumbs-down to the job of commentating on the next Coronation.

GOLD DIGGERS FLY IN

by Our South Africa Staff
Lunchtime O'Boers

A GROUP of happy-go-lucky prospectors flew into Britain from South Africa today hoping to "strike gold".

Their leader, a former High Court judge, Justice Cuckoldcarrot, had brought his whole family with him in order to mine the rich seam of the legendary Murdoch field.

Rich Seamy

"We are heading for Wapping," said the Judge, "as we have heard tales of vast wealth being acquired overnight by ordinary prospectors like ourselves."

Randy Kruger

The Judge has hired an experienced guide, Mr Max Clifford, who has helped many gold diggers to mine huge personal fortunes from the News of the World "lode".

"You have to sink pretty low," said Mr Clifford, "but when you reach rock bottom it's all worth it. There's great handfuls of money — you can just pick it up."

As his eyes shone with greed, the old 69er (as they are known) started to salivate.

"Only a few weeks ago this Spanish woman, Bienvenida was her name, she made a stack thanks to me. Now she's a Lady and appears in Hello!"

The Judge headed off with high hopes, accompanied by his family.

Silly Gold Fool

"I'm pretty sure we won't go home empty-handed. We don't mind if the work is dirty, so long as we get a vast sum from the press."

Since he became a recording star he employs that little man to have the blues for him"

HIRST'S MOTHER

TV HIGHLIGHTS

CIVILISATION
Part 94 of the Classic Series

Presented by the late Lord Clark

(Dapper connoisseur is seen standing in front of a picture of himself by Graham Sutherland)

Lord Clark *(for it is he):* What could be more agreeable than myself, surely a high point of civilisation, with my priceless art collection, my good works and my desire to inform and educate the masses by the new medium of television.

(Picks up copy of News of the World containing photograph of Alan Clark and headline MINISTER IN JUDGE'S WIFE AND DAUGHTERS LOVE ROMP*)*

Lord Clark: And in contrast, what could be more disagreeable than my son, surely a low point in civilisation, proof positive that the new dark ages are upon us. Alan, with his sordid affairs and his seedy arms dealing, his disregard for the truth and his sexual braggadocio… *(waves hand disparagingly)* All this reminds us how thin a veneer separates *us* from the savages. Thank goodness I am dead. Good night.

(Vivaldi music and credits)

GLYNDEBOURNE SHOCK

By Our Opera Staff **David Mellor di Radio**

OPERA lovers were last night shocked by a raunchy, no-holds-barred new production of Mozart's *Don Clarkoni*, in which the notorious libertine is portrayed as a former defence procurement minister who cannot keep his hands off anything in a skirt.

Act One opens with the boastful philanderer compiling an account of his conquests in many countries of the world. He sings the famous aria "Economico con l'actualité", while he casts admiring glances at the ankles of his elderly mistress Donna Maggi.

Coven Garden

But just when Don Clarkoni is feeling most pleased with himself, having sold 1003 copies of his Diario "in Spain alone", on to the stage come three masked figures, who accuse him of violating them all in the aria, "Tutti la Famiglia".

These are three discarded mistresses who have pursued him half way round the world in the hope of selling their story to a Sunday newspaper.

At the end of the final act, the mysterious statue of a judge comes to life, breathing vengeance on Clarkoni and threatening to horsewhip him.

Clarkoni refuses to repent and summons his lawyer, the legendary Bizet's George Carmen. It is too late. The Furies drag him down to hell.

CAST IN FULL

Don Clarkoni	LUCIANO PAVAROTTI
Donna Elvira Harkess	
	DAME KIRI TAKEAWAY
Donna Anna Harkess	
	DAME JANET BAKER
Donna Trelford Harkess	
	DAME PAMELLA BORDES
Donna Maggi	JESSYE NORMAN
The Judge	ROBERT TEAR
Man in Audience	DAVID FROSTRUP

The Saltwood Bedchamber Orchestra was conducted by MAX CLIFFORD CURZON.

COMING SOON: The Love of One Orange by S. Milligan.

CLARK'S WATERLOO

Not tonight Josephine. It's your mother's turn

From the *EuroJoke Book*

Page 94: Acceptable Jokes For Use In The Work Place

Section 7(b)

Q. How many Irishmen does it take to change a lightbulb?
A. Only one, because he is quite capable of doing it on his own.

> **Q.** Why did the Irish chicken cross the road?
> **A.** Because it had been sensible enough to make sure that there were no cars coming from either direction.

Knock, knock.
Who's there?

Gerry Adams
Gerry Adams who?

Gerry Adams is a very fine fellow who is striving earnestly for peace in very difficult circumstances.
(Under the British opt-out, this joke may only be told like an actor.)

New University Challenge
What viewers will see

(Silly music. Two teams sit either side of J. Paxman. One is captioned UNIVERSITY OF NEASDEN, FORMERLY THE NORTH CIRCULAR POLYTECHNIC, the other BROWNOSE COLLEGE, OXFORD)

Paxman *(for it is he)*: Good evening. Here is your starter for ten. Who is the central character in Shakespeare's play *Hamlet*?

(Buzzer sounds)

Voice Over: Wibble, Neasden, reading Media Studies and Counselling...

Wibble: Richard the Third?

Paxman: Oh really! Are you seriously suggesting that Richard the Third is the answer to the question? You are pathetic...

Wibble: Er... Sorry, sir.

Paxman: I'm going to offer it to Brownose.

(Buzzer sounds)

Voice Over: Chenevix-Twit, Brownose, reading English Literature...

Chenevix-Twit: Is it Oliver Twist?

Paxman: Come off it! Call yourself a student? There are people watching this programme to whom you *owe* a correct answer. Now come on!

Chenevix-Twit: Er... was it Middlemarch?

Paxman: I ask the questions here. Right, no marks for anyone. Back to Peter in the sandpit...

© Granada

SOLDIER ANT

WORKER ANT

CONSULTANT

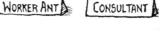

THE DAILY TELEGRAPH

LETTERS TO THE EDITOR

D-Day Reminiscences

From Sir Herbert Gussett

SIR,—Your readers may be interested to learn how two young men played their part in the great events which led to the liberation of Europe on 6 June 1944 — a story which for the past 50 years has never been told owing to the strictures of the Official Secrets Act.

It was in September 1939 that the two young heros in question — namely yours truly and his friend B. Frobisher — joined the colours in the West Sussex Dragoons (now, alas, absorbed in the Duchess of York's Northumberland and Southern Counties Light Infantry).

For five years we trained con-tinuously for the historic moment when allied troops would once again stand on the continent of Europe, as it languished under the jackboot of the filthy tyrant — ie the Hun, if in these days of so-called political correctness one is still allowed by M. Delors to call a spade a spade!

Through all those long years we prepared for the great day, training non-stop with a continual round of route marches, bayonet drill and kit inspections.

Finally in June 1944 the long-awaited day came, when our supreme Commander General Eisenhower uttered his immortal call to arms: "Let's go, boys!" Buffy and I situated building at the centre of the village to establish our where-at once leaped into our trusty Bren Carrier and prepared to join the endless queue of vehicles which was heading for the South Coast.

It was an astonishing sight which no one who was there on that day will ever forget. Women and children stood in their gardens by the roadside, waving Union Jacks with cries of "Godspeed".

Unfortunately we had barely advanced ten yards on our historic mission when our erstwhile trusty Bren carrier came to an unplanned halt due to what we ascertained was a lack of petrol. By the time Buffy had returned from HQ with the necessary fuel, the convoy had moved on and we were forced to travel alone across unknown terrain.

As your older readers may recall, in the emergency conditions of wartime, all signposts had been removed for the duration to confuse the enemy. Thus it was that the following morning, at approximately 1200 hours, we found ourselves entering a small hamlet. Seeing the place deserted, we made our way into a strategically abouts and to get a map reference for our allotted embarkation point, eg Dover. It transpired, as luck would have it, that we had alighted upon the village hostelry, the sign of which had been taken down for the same security reason as the signposts (see above). Behind the bar stood the landlord, the late Mr Zechariah Balon, who having assured himself that we were not German spies by asking us to name the winner of the Derby in 1938, informed us that we were over 150 miles to the west of our PE (Port of Embarkation). He suggested that, before attempting to rejoin our unit, we might care to revive our morale by sampling some of his much-prized home-made elderflower whisky at a reasonably price. Col. Frobisher and myself accepted his proposal with alacrity and to cut a long story short, we have been here ever since.

SIR H. GUSSET
The Lamb and Flag
Somewhere in South West
England
Dorset.

HISTORIC D-DAY SOUVENIR

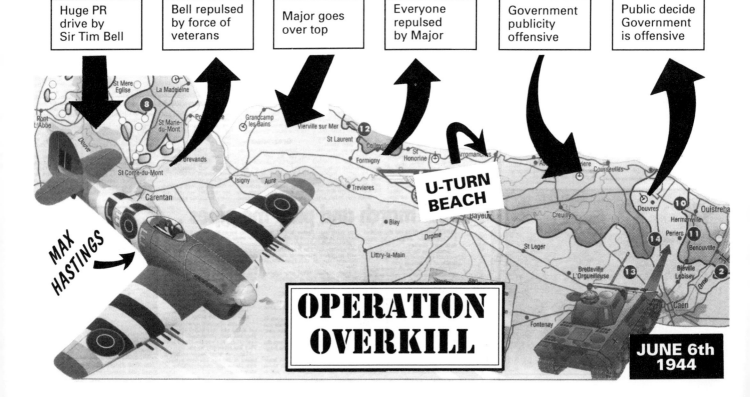

Huge PR drive by Sir Tim Bell | Bell repulsed by force of veterans | Major goes over top | Everyone repulsed by Major | Government publicity offensive | Public decide Government is offensive

U-TURN BEACH

MAX HASTINGS

OPERATION OVERKILL

JUNE 6th 1944

Notes & Queries

A service by our readers for our readers (as seen in all other newspapers)

QUESTION: Why was D-Day so called?

☐ I MUST take issue with J Fenby in your last issue, who claimed erroneously that the 'D' in D-day was due to a typing error by Churchill's secretary Cpl. Moneypenny of the WRAC, and should have read 'O-Day' for Operation Overlord. Surely every schoolboy (and indeed schoolgirl) knows that the 'D' was chosen as apart of a plan to confuse the Germans by fooling them into thinking that the invasion was going to take place in December — hence 'D' for the month in question. — *Capt. M. Willoughby, Uffcombe.*

☐ THERE is no mystery about D-Day. Originally Eisenhower had drawn up a series of possible dates for the invasion. Each was given a code-letter — eg A-Day was March 14th 1943, B-Day was October 12th 1943, and C-Day was May 1st 1944 — and so on till Z-Day which was 31st December 1960. As luck would have it, the weather forecast for the day code-lettered D was June 6th 1944, and the rest is history. — *Victor Maltby, Bognor Regis.*

☐ THE 'D' in D-Day, as all we Germans learned in school, stood for "Der Tag", ie "the day" in German. When the news of the Allied invasion came through, we were all overjoyed as we realised it would soon mean the liberation of our country from people like my father. — *A. Goebbels, Berlin.*

QUESTION: is it true that all the plans for D-Day were sent by German secret agents to their Nazi masters via the Daily Telegraph crossword?

☐ THIS is perfectly true. The compiler of the Telegraph crossword, Quisling, was a German emigré who had met Churchill in his club a few weeks before the invasion. In typically expansive mood, the prime minister explained his

masterplan for the reconquest of Europe, which Quisling in due course incorporated into his crosswords of June 1-5. The answers were as follows:

ACROSS. 1. Watch out. 5. Adolf. 8. Allies 10. Will 12. Invade 14. Omelette 17. Normandy 20. June 21. Sixth 28. Salamander. — *Kevin Cholmondeley-Farquharson, Blandford.*

QUESTION: What does the word 'Day' mean in D-Day?

☐ DAY was the name of a popular American singer Doris (or D) Day, who entertained the troops with such songs as Top Secret Love and Hitler Get Your gun. She was known as the "Forces Sweetheart" and inevitably the great day was named after her. — *C. Day-Lewis, Puddleton.*

☐ I HAVE never heard such nonsense. D-Day was named after me. — *Daniel Day-Lewis, Hollywood, Ireland.*

NEXT WEEK'S QUESTIONS: Is it true that the Aztecs invented the Lilo? Are snakes colour-blind? Why is the periodic table so-called? How did Mariella Frostrup get that column in the Sunday Times?

KIDDIES' EURO-CORNER

MAKE YOUR OWN ELECTION BROADCAST

What You Need

- ● Aerial film of White Cliffs of Dover.
- ● Elgar-style patriotic music.
- ● Statistics showing Britain either coming out of recession or not.
- ● Black-and-white film of D-Day.
- ● Man in suit explaining advantages of being in Europe while at the same time sticking up for Britain's interests.
- ● Pie-chart showing increase or decrease in jobs as appropriate.
- ● Slogan — e.g. Putting Britain First In Europe.
- ● Hotline number.
- ● Vote Conservative/Labour/Lib-Dem (Labour).

Poetry Corner

In Memoriam Lady Wemyss and Mr George Peppard, Star of The A-Team.

So.
Farewell then
Lady Wemyss,
104.

You were the last
Surviving godchild
Of Queen
Victoria.

And farewell also
George Peppard
Of TV's
A-Team.

You had nothing
Much
In common.
But death
Has now united you.

E.J. Thribb (17½)

E.J. Thribb was recently runner-up in the election of the new Oxford Professor of Poetry. He polled 0 votes.

THAT Tony Blur David Frost INTERVIEW IN FULL

Sir David Frostrup: Hello, good morning and welcome.

Tony Blur: I think it's too early to say that.

Sir Davidella Frostrup: So if you become Prime Minister will you be committed to full employment?

Phony Blur: Obviously we want to have a society, David, where everyone has an opportunity to work, and the Labour Party is committed to this.

Sir Kellogg's Frostrups: And when exactly do you envisage that happening? Can you set a date or a target for this?

Tony Blahblah: I can't possibly give a date for answering that question, but what I *can* do is give you a firm commitment to repeat my previous answer about the Labour Party's commitment to the sort of society that I mentioned earlier. *(Smiles angelically)*

Sir David Fisticuffs: Super! But what about the other candidates for the Labour leadership? Do you see John Prescott as a threat?

Tony Hot-Blair: John Prescott and I have no differences of opinion over anything. He thinks he should be leader and I think I should be. We are as one on this one. *(Smiles again)*

Sir David Firstup: Should you end up in Number Ten Downing Street, Tony, could you set a firm date for me getting a peerage?

Fuzzy Blair: It is far too early to get up and appear on this programme.

(This continues in same vein until Disney Club, when viewers switch on)

"so, to recap: your parents are both tossers, your teachers are all f**ckers, and I'm a four-eyed shirt-lifter whose car is being 'done over' as we speak"

GRAND SUMMER PHOTO BUBBLE COMPETITION

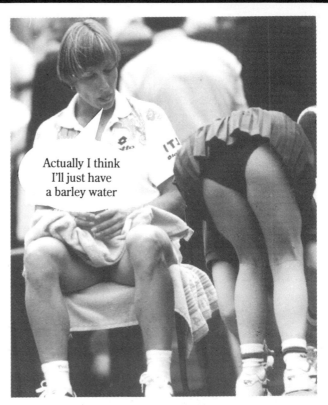

Actually I think I'll just have a barley water

⭐ **WINNER: N. Ferris.**

Thanks to all three hundred readers for sending in *"No balls please"*, *"15, love?"* *"I've got to leave this behind"*, *"I'm going to look up my old friends at Wimbledon"*, *"It's a thigh break"*, *"You should have a Czech-up"*, and tons more filth that cannot be repeated in a family satirical magazine.

Special Mention. The bottom saying *"I think Britain can produce a world-class tennis player"*.

Lines on the Historic Failure of The Irish Football Team to Win the 1994 World Cup

 by William Rees-Maradonagall

'Twas in the year nineteen hundred and ninety-four
That Jack Charlton's lads set off for the distant American
shore.
All Irishmen entertained a noble dream
That when the final whistle blew, theirs would be the
winning team.

Not only in the Emerald Isle were their supporters found,
But all over Britain the cry of "Good Old Paddies" did
resound
For neither England nor Scotland had qualified,
Not even Wales — their hopes too had sadly died.

And so it was that, led by Big Jack Charlton,
We all watched their triumphal progress on either BBC
or Carlton.
For the first round they beat Italy, thus raising
everyone's hopes,
A 1-Nil victory over the lads from the land of the Popes.

Next for the chop were the lads from the land of the fjord,
But unfortunately for St Jack no one from either side
scored.
Next came the Mexicans, from the land of the sombrero
And this time the Irish point tally was unfortunately zero.

Twice their opponents found the net,
Which made Charlton's heroes an increasingly unlikely
bet.
Nevertheless, they had just done enough to qualify for
the next round

Where they faced the lads from Holland in an enormous
baseball ground.
All over Britain the excitement was running high
Whilst in Dublin's fair city not a single mouth was dry.
The commentators all agreed to a man
That the Dutch were weak in defence and would be an
also-ran.

But alas and alack they had reckoned without the
luckless goal-keeper Bonner
For when he let in the second goal, Ireland were a gonner.
From Kerry to Galway, from Donegal to Cork,
From Kilburn to Camden, from Long Kesh to New York,

Where once the bars had been filled with cheers
There was nothing now but weeping and tears.
But after a jar or two, more thoughtful counsel prevailed
And Irishmen everywhere realised that their team had far
from failed.

The important thing was that they had achieved so much
And were unlucky to have been slaughtered by the
superior Dutch.
As even the great Jimmy Hill pronounced on TV
"The lads can hold their heads up high, if you ask me."

And so they returned in triumph to the town of the Liffey
And everyone forget that their performance had actually
been rather iffy.

©William Rees-McDonegal

Poetry Corner

In Memoriam John Wain.

So. Farewell then
John Wain.

You were not the famous
One.

E.J. Thribb (17¾)

The Daily Hellograph

FRIDAY, JULY 1, 1994

Pop Singer Loses Court Case

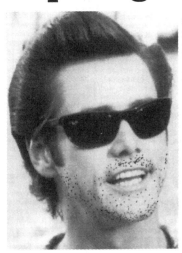

A WELL-KNOWN pop singer, Boy George Michael Jackson, has lost a £20 million case in the High Court, it was revealed today.

Hundreds of fans (Sid and Doris Hastings) had been waiting outside the court for 48 hours to hear whether their idol had been successful in his bid to be released from his contract to the multi-million pound leisure conglomerate Lemsweat International.

When the verdict was announced, many fans fainted and burst into tears. "This is one of the most tragic days in history," said Jackson's manager, Peter Stibbins, after the case.

The implications of yesterday's verdict are likely to send shock waves throughout the civilised world.

"When a major artist of Jackson's stature cannot break his contract," said one senior music industry figure, disc jockey Rap Snorkel, "then we see the Apocalypse staring us in the face."

Lady Thatcher was last night unavailable for comment.

On Other Pages: Editorial p. 15; Michael Case — Will He Appeal to European Court of Human Rights? p. 20; The Boy Jackson I Knew by Simon Heffer p. 18.

Night Of Long Knives At Daily Goodbyegraph

by Our Media Staff Jane Thynne-Stuff

IN AN imaginative bid to halt his declining circulation, the most courageous newspaper editor of this or any other time, Max "Hitler" Hastings, last night sacked several of his closest colleagues.

"Our aim", he said, "is to give the *Telegraph* a new look. What we need is more women in senior positions, more female columnists and more sex, violence, knickers and showbiz gossip. Our research shows that this is what young readers want — not boring articles about D-Day by Brig. Trumper-Smythe and myself."

Hitler Hastings is 72.

Baronet Shoots Owl

AN East Anglian baronet, Sir Hugh Montgomery-Massacrebird, was yesterday sentenced to five hours community service for shooting a rare Red-Bearded Owl which, under the EC Bird Directive, is now a protected species.

The owl, *Strix barbarossa*, is believed to have been the last surviving example of a species once common in Norfolk.

Said Sir Hugh: "This bird was a bloody nuisance, and kept me awake with its hooting while I was watching the World Cup."

Pix p.14. Should Sir Hugh have shot the owl? Ring Telegraph Owl-line on 0898-222.

UP 35%!

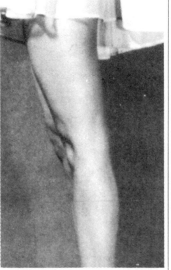

OUR proprietor's wife yesterday raised her skirt by 35 per cent. "That should compensate for the fall in our share price!" quipped a jubilant Conrad Blackadder, the Telegraph's Canadian proprietor.

Why This Man Should Be Next PM

by Max Hastings

IF THE Conservative Party wishes to recover from its present misfortunes, one obvious remedy is immediately available.

They should get rid of this Major chappie and bring in my friend Nicko Soames as prime minister.

Not only is Nick a first-class shot and raconteur. He is, as this picture shows, a man with the common touch whose Yorkshire pudding-eating has deservedly won him a place in the Guinness Book of Records under the heading "The World's Fattest Man".

The *Daily Telegraph* has long championed Mr Soames's claims to the highest office, which is perhaps why its circulation has fallen by 300,000 copies in the last six months.

On Other Pages: Why This Clubbable Bon Viveur Would Win The Women's Vote, by Veronica Wadley, p. 16

Ark of Covenant Found in St Cakes Cricket Pavilion

By Our Salesroom Staff **Linford Christies**

THE HEADMASTER of St Cakes, Mr R.R. Kipling, was said to be overjoyed yesterday at the sale at the record price of £300 million of the Judaic artefact known as the Ark of the Covenant.

Missing for thousands of years the Ark came to light during a refurbishment of the famous public school's cricket pavilion where it had been used for storing pads, boxes and other cricketing impedimenta.

Amazing Box

The Ark was spotted by an old boy, Norrington Rameses-Smith, who is now a director of the auction house, Gnomebys.

"I couldn't believe my eyes", he said. "The boys who frequented the pavilion (known as 'The Pavver') for illicit smoking had even used the Ark as an ashtray."

Speaking from a luxury cruise liner in the Bahamas, the Headmaster, Mr Kipling, told reporters: "This money will not change the character of the school at all. Partly because they won't see any of it."

St Cakes is 107.

Two milkshakes and a Wagon Wheel while you're there Hammurabi Minor

BRITANNIA TO BE PHASED OUT

by Our Yacht Staff **Lunchtime O'Hoy**

BRITANNIA, the floating island off the coast of France, is to be phased out by 1996 it was revealed today.

Formerly the symbol of Empire across the globe, this once-proud island is now too expensive to maintain as an independent concern.

Britannia Waves Goodbye

European nations have no interest in Britannia, which they regard as an outdated relic of the past.

However, one possibility is that the island will be sold to an Arab consortium and turned into a tourist attraction.

Another plan is to sell it to an American tycoon who would reconstruct it as a Theme Park in Texas, complete with Royal processions, rail-strikers and Gay Rights marches through Trafalgar Square on Sunday afternoons.

GCSE Core Curriculum Statutory Assessment Task I, Grade 10

EEC/421/DoEduc   July 1994

MORAL STUDIES Paper II

Candidates are expected to try at least one question.

1. You are asked to imagine the following real-life scenario:

A set of ovaries has been transplanted from the body of a dead divorcee into the body of a teenage would-be single parent to enable her to exercise her basic consumer right to have a child by artificial insemination.

After the child is born the mother, due to the trauma of the experience, exercises her basic human right to change her mind. The baby is then taken into care by social workers, and fostered out to two lesbians on income support, who enjoy a stable relationship. Unfortunately, owing to the negative social pressures inherent in our current society, the stable relationship of the lesbian foster-parents breaks down.

Candidates are asked to write an assessment paper for the Child Support Agency detailing all the available options as to whom the Agency should pursue to enforce payment for the upkeep of the child.

Should it be (a) the errant husband of the original donor of the ovaries? (b) the inseminee, who is also on income support? (c) the lesbian foster-mother? (d) the lesbian foster-father? (e) the taxpayer. Clue: the answer is (e).

RGJ

COMMUTER FURY AS RAILMEN GO BACK

by Our BR Staff **Lady Paddington Bore** (Margaret Jay)

MILLIONS of angry commuters were enraged yesterday when they found trains running as normal, forcing them to return to work.

"You think you know where you are," said one City man, "ie, out in the garden with a Pimms watching Wimbledon on the portable TV, when suddenly these bastards decide to go back to work."

"I don't know what the country's coming to," said a Bromley secretary. "It's almost back to the bad old days of the Eighties, when everyone had to work every day."

"It's not our fault," explained an unrepentant Union leader, Jimmy Knapp. "My members have got to work sometime, to earn some money. It is our democratic right to work, which we are prepared to go on strike for if needs be."

RUMOURS THAT THE TUNNEL WOULD BRING CLOSER LINKS WITH FRANCE SENT PANIC ROUND THE VILLAGE POND

WAS GRAHAM GREENE A WOMAN?

by Christopher Whohee
(author of *The Annotated Cheque Stubs Of Graham Greene*)

A SENSATIONAL new book about author Graham Greene, the seventeenth published this week, reveals that the Catholic novelist may well have been a woman.

Author Prof. Norman Toshberger puts forward astonishing new evidence which suggests that Greene, in addition to being a senior officer in the KGB, was a transvestite nun who enjoyed having public sex on the altars of more than 400 cathedrals while being stabbed repeatedly with burning pokers.

Among the Professor's other findings about Greene:

● The novelist stole the plots of all his novels from Jeffrey Archer.

● His real name was Natasha Wheen.

● He had an affair with Josef Stalin when the Soviet dictator was studying to be a priest at a Jesuit seminary.

● He often went to *Spectator* lunches when in London and once met Jeffrey Bernard.

Prof. Toshberger's revelations will be welcomed by the *Daily Telegraph* as a way to fill up its pages for the next two months *(shurely 'will be welcomed by scholars for the light they shed on the brooding moral ambiguity of Britain's greatest novelist'?)*.

Yes! It's Islington Person Rhyming Slang!

Georgian Square	**Tony Blair**
Wife called Cherie	**Canonbury**
One of us!	**No. 19 Bus**
Islington Person	**Clive And-erson**
Stripped pine door	**Clause Four**
Louis Blom-Cooper	**Food at Granita's super!**
Sons of Toil	**Virgin olive oil**
Francis Wheen	**Stuffed Aubergine**
Salmon Fishcakes	**Martin Jaques**
Geoff Robertson QC	**Glass of Chablis**
Chardonnay	**Minimum pay**
Screen on the Green	**Where Mike Ignatieff's seen**
Charles Moore	**Lives next door** *(shurely shome mishtake? Ed)*

Apology To Mr. J. Major

In common with all other newspapers we may in recent months have given the impression that the Prime Minister, the Rt. Hon. John Major, was in some way a hopeless, dithering, ineffectual wimp who was totally in the thrall of his European colleagues and was drifting aimlessly into total subservience to Brussels. Headlines such as "MAJOR IS USELESS" or "MAJOR IS TOTALLY USELESS" or "NO BUT MAJOR REALLY IS TOTALLY USELESS", may have inadvertently contributed to the misunderstanding that Mr. Major really was totally useless.

However we now realise that following Mr. Major's decision to object to some fat Belgian getting some Euro-job, the Prime Minister is now the most heroic, courageous and decisive leader this country has known since Winston Churchill. We furthermore accept that in standing up to all those ghastly Frogs, Belgies and Huns, Mr. Major has taken on the mantle of Horatio Nelson, the Duke of Wellington and Henry V.

We apologise unreservedly for any confusion our previous articles may have caused, and would like to take this opportunity to ask our readers to vote Conservative.

World of Soccer

KNEE EYES WORLD CUP STARS

by **E.I. Erewego**, Our Man At The Rosebowl Sitting Next To An American Asking What A Goal Is

"He's a winosaur"

THE WORLD of soccer was rocked to its foundations when Ron Knee, the 57-year-old manager of Neasden FC, told reporters that he had put in a bid for the whole Brazilian team. The tight-lipped supremo explained: "They are match-winners, every one of them, and they are going to swap the yellow jersey of Brazil for the famous black and white hooped strip of Neasden."

Baggio: Neasden bound?

BRAZIL NUT

Experts were amazed that the recently relegated North London club with reported debts of £10 million and a jail sentence hanging over its chairman could be in the marketplace for the world's top eleven players, but Ron Knee made his position clear.

"The Brazil side we are looking at is the World Cup winning side of 1958. You are going to see names like Aristotle, Hebrides, Georgino, Carlos Santana, Bibi, Ricardo Salamanca, Suez, Filio Oranjeboom and his brother Ronsōn, Frostrup, and Whittam-Smith."

Although some of Knee's shopping list are in their 70s and many are dead, the ashen-faced mastermind of the Neasden squad refuses to be downcast.

"I have put £25 on the table. They can take it or leave it. But one thing is for sure. Neasden will be fielding a world class side, with the samba rhythms echoing around our all-seater (one) stadium for the big kick-off in August."

SUBBUTEO ITALIAN VERSION

LATE SCORE

Pre-Season Charity Exhibition Friendly (sponsored by The Sofabed Company)

FC Neasden	0
Dollis Hill	0

After extra time and penalty shoot-out there was still no score

---

PRIVATE EYE EXCLUSIVE

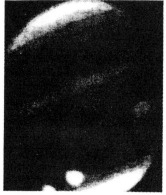

Before

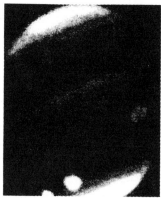

After

MOST DRAMATIC SPACE PICTURES EVER SEEN

by Our Man In Space **TV's Patrick Bore (no relation)**

YES, make no mistake about it, these are the most astonishing photos I have ever seen!

Look carefully at these two pictures. The one on the left shows the planet Jupiter as it looked at 9.46 last night.

Only seconds later it is hit head on by a piece of the comet Shoesize-Eleven 250,000 times the size of Planet Earth, with a force the equivalent of 10 billion Hiroshimas.

As the picture on the right clearly shows, the universe will never be the same again.

Last night astronomers were jubilant. "We can now see how the Universe began," said Professor Branestawm of the University of Heath Robinson in Pasodoble, California. "We know everything now."

MAN IN THE EYE

The Lunar Veteran Whose Historic Mission

Changed His Life For Good

"WHEN you've been to the moon, nothing in life ever quite matches up to the experience."

So says Colonel "Buzz" Cow, the first cow to jump over the moon.

Interviewed in his California home, Colonel Cow talks frankly about his problems on returning to earth.

"I started drinking heavily. I went into therapy and eventually I found religion."

But the Colonel, now a retired milk salesman in Palm Springs, says that his experience was typical of all those involved in the moon mission.

"The pressure told on us all. The Dish and Spoon split up soon afterwards and the Dish more or less slept his way through the entire cutlery drawer. The little dog hasn't laughed since and has become a Mormon. The cat who orchestrated the historic moonjump is now in the Betty Ford Clinic on a detoxification programme."

But the cow still believes that the enterprise was worthwhile.

"We should be endeavouring to build on my achievement," he told us, "and put a sheep on Mars."

ENGLAND CAPTAIN IN DIRT SCANDAL

by Our Political Staff **Bruce Atherton**

BELEAGUERED England skipper John Majorton last night admitted that he had been found "with dirt on his hands".

TV evidence showed that members of his team had been cheating regularly in order to win large sums of money from businessmen.

Very Seamy

"The use of pay-dirt is not technically illegal," he said, "and anyway everyone does it. All you do is put a lot of filthy lucre in your pocket just in case you fancy it."

Critics last night refused to accept Majorton's explanation. "He will stay on for a short time," said one insider, "but if his team continues to lose so badly he will stay on again." *(Shurely shome mishtake?)*

LATE SCORE

Brian Lara £300,000,000 not out, retired rich.

Keith Floyd's Recipe for Divorce

Ingredients
Wine
More Wine
Lots More Wine
Even More Wine

— ✳ —

Instructions
Drink the above

NEXT WEEK:
Poached Ego on an Empty bed

"They're not going to like this at Wisden"

KINNOCK JOINS EC — TRANSLATORS DEMAND OVERTIME

by Our Man in Brussels **Ian Sprout MP**

TODAY hundreds of simultaneous translators walked out of the EC Commission after their first morning of dealing with a speech by the new £2-million-a-year British Commissioner, Mr Neil Kinnock. A spokesman said: "We have had enough. It is unreasonable to expect anyone to cope with this sort of workload."

WHAT THE DELEGATES HEARD

FRENCH

Mesdames, Messieurs, je suis totallement et absolument et totallement absolument enchanté d'être ici à Brussels. Mon enchantement est totalle, absolut et absolument totallement absolut, etcétéra...

GERMAN

Mein Herren und Damen, ich bin totallich und utterlich und utterlich and totallich gemütlichfahrenweisenwöllen grübbenoberdermoon... vorsprung durch technik... (etcetera)

ITALIAN

Signori, Signorini, sono totallimenti y absolutimenti contenti essare Comissione di Europeani quattro formagio multo fribi y sono absolutimenti y totallimenti et absolutimenti totalli... *(continued in 94 other languages)*

"Before you take my daughter's hand in marriage I've set up a little test for you"

PETER McLIE

The Return of the World's Worst Columnist

ISN'T IT time the Labour Party found a new leader? We're all sick and tired of the old Welsh windbag bleating on. No wonder Mrs Thatcher is still in Downing Street if Neil Kinnock is all she has to contend with.

They should sack no-good Neil and replace him with a bonny Scotsman with a good head for figures.

Step forward Mrs Margaret Beckett!

● *What happened to the good old British summer?*

When I was a wee bairn the sun shone down from cloudless blue skies, as we feasted on strawberries and haggis on the golden sands of Auchtermuchty.

But this summer, the experts tell me, has been the coldest and wettest on record.

No wonder my friend A.N. Wilson has taken to bicycling around in a long woolly scarf and galoshes!

I HAVE recently discovered an extraordinary thing.

If you get in your car and drive far enough in one direction, you will eventually come to a huge stretch of water.

I have even thought of a name for it — the trouser press.

John Walsh, former literary editor of the *Sunday Times* and current editor of the *Independent*'s prestigious Saturday Review, talks to the actress **Miss Elle McPherson** about her role in the forthcoming cinematic work "Sirens".

Cor... phew... blimey... look at the legs on that... whorr!!... eh?... wouldn't kick her out of bed for eating crackers... honestly... bloody 'ell... is it me or is it

hot in here or what?... Wahay!!... I reckon I'm in here!! (Cont. p.94)

THE NUMBER TEN RED HERRING

A New Short Story from the Master Taleteller of Our Times

Jeffrey Archer

"GOOD AFTERNOON, Prime Minister. So good of you to come to my garden party in my luxury, £850,000 riverside home at Granchester, famous for having been once lived in by another great English writer, Rupert Brooke."

The speaker was a tanned, handsome, rich, talented former Olympic athlete who had given up his career as an astronaut to devote his life to helping those less fortunate than himself, ie the Conservative Party.

"Hello, Lord Archer, it was very gracious of you to ask me and my wife Norma to your party."

The speaker was none other than the Prime Minister of England, John Major.

"I think you know everyone here," Lord Archer beamed, as he shook the British premier warmly by the hand.

"Lord Parkinson, Lord Howe, Lord Tebbit, Sir Timothy Rice, Mr Torvill and Miss Dean, the world-famous ice-skating duo, and of course Miss Mariella Frostrup, who needs no introduction."

The prime minister smiled and looked across the manicured lawns to where the world-famous River Cam wound its way lazily through ancient water meadows towards the distant sea.

"Ah," sighed Mr Major, "this is really England at its best, Jeffrey; I congratulate you." The famous novelist laughed heartily, and saw his opportunity to whisper a very special request in the PM's ear. "Can I be Chairman of the Party?"

By a brilliant twist, the master storyteller has provided this story with four alternative endings. These are:

A. At this moment, two burly policemen elbowed their way through the crowd of celebrities and brusquely commanded the distinguished novelist to come down to the station to help them with their enquiries about insider dealing.

B. The prime minister choked on his piece of Mary Archer's world-famous Shepherd's Pie, and said "You must be joking, Jeff. I'm unpopular enough as it is without having you around."

C. The Prime Minister woke up in a cold sweat and turned to his wife. "I've just had the most ghastly nightmare. I dreamed we went to one of Jeffrey's awful garden parties and he asked me to make him Chairman of the Party."

D. The reader, having got this far, gets so irritated by this drivel that he turns to his wife and says: "I'm not going to lug this all the way home. Let's leave it in the hotel bedroom to ruin someone else's holiday."

NOW 5p

The Daily Hellograph

NEWSPAPER OF THE YEAR

NOW 5p

FINAL

FRIDAY, AUGUST 26, 1994

'A'-Level Results Soar To New Record

**By Our Education Correspondent
JANE THYKKE**

A young girl of the type who yesterday was going through the trauma of waiting for her 'A'-Level results

THE GOVERNMENT today claimed that the 105 per cent pass-rate for this year's 'A'-Levels showed that its educational reforms were "paying off".

The results show that more candidates this year passed 'A'-Levels than actually took the exams, setting a new world record.

"This shows that Britain is now the best-educated nation in the world," claimed junior education minister Eric Fourthform.

A Level Playing Field

"There were 2.5 million A Grades awarded this year," said Mr Fourthrate, "an increase of 417 per cent on last year, which was itself a record year."

The subjects in which pupils achieved the highest grades were:
● media studies (television)
● physical education (football)
● sociology (video nasties)
● communications (pop music)
● information technology (Nintendo)
● consumer economics (Big Macs)

"The only disappointment," continued Mr Forthbridge, "came in science subjects, where only two candidates (Mungal and Punam Bonkerjee of the Roy Hattersley School for Girls, Birmingham) passed Mathematics and no one at all passed Physics. But since no one is going to get any jobs anyway, it hardly matters, does it?"

An example of the type of 'A'-Level paper in which Britain leads the world can be seen below.

"I want to make A-Levels easy enough for me to get one"

EXAM REFORM

RGJ

A Level June 1994   EC/104

Media Studies (Television)

Candidates need only attempt one question, and then only if they feel like it.

1. Who is the star of Roseanne? Is it:
   a) Roseanne
   b) Ena Sharples
   c) Mariella Frostrup.

2. Have you ever watched any of the following?
   a) Red Dwarf
   b) Rab C. Nesbitt
   c) The Bandung File.

3. "Danny Baker is great." Discuss.

4. Imagine if for some crazy reason you got up really early. Would you watch:
   a) The Big Breakfast with Chris Evans
   b) GMTV with Judy and Ron
   c) News At Ten with Trevor Barbados
   d) The Bandung File with Tariq Ali.
   Time Allowed 4 Hours.

Jersey murderers were Old Cakeians

THE TWO boys who were yesterday found guilty of hacking their parents to death were among the most distinguished recent alumni of St Cakes, the £42,000-a-year Berkshire public school.

Ronald and Reginald Kraye-Smythe were at St Cakes in the 1980s. Ronald was Head of School in 1986, and his younger brother Reginald was head of Sutcliffe House two years later.

The brothers are remembered with affection by the then-headmaster, Mr J.L.R. Kipling, who said yesterday: "Both boys were model pupils and murdered no one while they were here. At least, not to my knowledge."

Another St Cake's figure who knew them well was their house matron, Miss Rosa Klebb-Trumpington. "Ronnie and Reggie were always favourites of mine," she said yesterday. "I remember when they came fifth and sixth one year in the Sock Race."

The Sock Race is an old St Cakes tradition, dating back to 1951. Teams from two houses try to kill each other in a sea of mud, using only their socks as weapons.

The last boy to die in "Sockers" was in 1961.

"Doctor I'm worried – my husband spends the whole day lying in bed"

FROM THE NEW APOCRYPHA

THE BOOK OF ENOCH

AND lo, there was dwelling in the land of the Briton-ites a man whose name was Enoch.

2. And he was heavy with age, even unto four score years and ten.

3. And the children of Brit-on had for long years harkened not to the counsels of Enoch, saying amongst themselves "Verily, he is wash-ed up".

4. For, in former times, Enoch had lifted up his voice to prophesy against the children of Ham, namely those who had come from the lands of Jam-aica, Barb-a-dos, Trin-i-dad and those other lands where they worship the god Gan-ja and dance to the sound of the drum which is made of steel. *(Get on with it. God.)*

5. For he had prophesied, saying that unless the dwellers in Brix-ton and Hands-worth and those within the gate that is called Notting Hill returneth whence they came, yea even to Af-rica, then the River Tiber shall foam with much blood, even as the poet hath foretold.

6. I, Enoch, say all these things shall come to pass. So spake Enoch.

7. But, as it happeneth, he was quite wrong. And they cometh not to pass at all.

8. And Enoch was utterly cast out, even into outer darkness.

9. And he was no longer permitted to take part in the councils of the nation, even amongst the wise men, and one woman you've never heard of, who appeareth on Any Questions, which tonight cometh from the Freemasons' Hall, Doncaster.

10. And when Enoch had been thus shunned by the people, he remaineth in the wilderness for forty years. And his name was quite forgotten.

11. And lo, wouldst thou believe it, Enoch suddenly riseth up in the season that is called silly and attempteth an comeback.

12. And Enoch cried aloud, harken unto me, for a vision hath been vouchsafed to me that your eyes may be opened, and that once more my words shall be heard in the land, at the sixth hour, at the ninth hour and even on News At The Tenth Hour, when they shall be proclaimed by the man that is called Bar-ab-a-dos.

13. And Enoch spake unto them, saying: "Everyone hath got it wrong, saving me alone. Our Lord, whom ye call crucified, was no such thing.

14. "I say unto you that he was put to death by stoning."

15. And the Chief Priests and Elders mocked him, saying: "How knowest thou these things?"

16. And Enoch addressed them, saying: "There is a book in which all these things are written, even though it hath not yet been discovered and no man hath read it."

17. And they laughed him to scorn, and took up bread rolls, even the Bread Sea Rolls, and cast them at Enoch, shouting: "Thou art an old loony, as we have known all along."

18. And Enoch once again found himself in the darkness that is outer.

Here endeth the Book of Enoch.

The Royal Dynasty of Pop

Wedding Of The Century

Mary-Lou Presley

How They Are Related

Michael Jackson

King Elvis the Pelvis of Graceland	Peter Pan of Neverland
Queen Priscilla Presley of Dallas	Pan's People
Rev John Presley	Rev Jesse Jackson
Rev Ian Presley	General Stonewall Jackson
Rev Presley Baxendale QC	Princess Michael of Jackson
5 Million Kids Called Elvis Born In 1958	Radio Jackson Five Live
Elvis Costello	Jackson and the Beanstalk
Abbott and Costello	Jackson and the Moonwalk
Dianne Abbott	**Mariella Frostrup** *(shurely shome mishtake?)*

CIVIL ENGINEER

WOULD YOU MIND, AWFULLY, IF I BUILT A BRIDGE HERE?

knife

That Wedding Menu in full

Jailhouse Rock Salmon Served On A Bed Of Young Boys
(shurely 'Lettuce'? Ed)

NEW WORDS

with Philip Howard

JAGGER
vb. int. To dance about in an exhibitionistic fashion when far too old. E.g. "Please stop jaggering, Dad, it's embarrassing." (*Adrian Mole's Guide To Provence*, 1994)

KNAPP
n. Scots vernacular. To spend the day asleep in the garden instead of going to work. E.g. "I think I'll have a knapp this Wednesday, dear."

LITTLEJOHN
n. Cockney slang. One who affects manner and opinions of a London cab-driver to make money. E.g. "Did you see that littlejohn on TV last night? I agree with him about those lesbians." (LBC Phone-In, 1994)

HURLEY
n. Woman who impulsively undresses in public. E.g. "What a shameless hurley — doon tae her knockers again *(surely 'knickers'? Ed.)*." (*The New Dr Finlay's Casebook*, 1995)

FROSTRUP
n. Fictitious woman made up by satirical magazine in order to fill pages.

This Week's Honorary Degrees

MR WINSTON SILCOTT, 35, seen here receiving an Honorary Doctorate in Civil Law from the University of Calcutt (formerly Gatwick Polytechnic).

He is pictured with the writer and broadcaster Ms Mariella Frostrup, who was made a Doctor of Letters for her contribution to literature.

The Rocky Horror Mastermind Final Service from Coventry Cathedral

President: *(For it is Magnus Magnusson)* What is thy name and occupation?

(At this point the man with the beard shall be seated and shall reply.)

Beardie: I an N or M and I am a Polytechnic Lecturer. *(Or he may say "I am a Librarian". Or he may say "I am a Retired Civil Servant".)*

President: And what is thy Specialist Subject?

Beardie: The popular songs of Cliff Richard (post-Shadows). *(Or he may say "The Life and Works of the Russian Beat Poet Michael Horovitz". Or he may say "English Cheeses 1973-1974".)*

(There shall be a moment of silence during which the congregation may cough.)

President: N or M You have two minutes on your chosen subject, starting now.

THE RESPONSES

President: Which Greek Goddess was symbolised by a gerbil?

N or M: Pass.

President: In the Periodical Table, which element is denoted by the letters "Zt"?

N or M: Strontium.

President: No. Gnomium.

(At this point N or M will tut and roll his eyes as if he knew the answer all along. The President then continues in similar vein until a bleep is sounded.)

THE DISMISSAL

President: As I have started, so shall I finish. Why is a TV quiz show being held in Coventry Cathedral?

The Bishop: We needeth the money.

All: Amen-with-Beards.

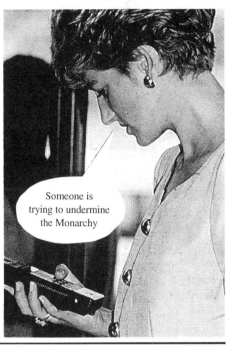
A Dentist Writes

As a dentist I am often asked: "Do mercury amalgam fillings cause Alzheimer's Disease?" I always reply: "No, of course not. It's a lot of typical journalistic scaremongering."

The patient then asks me, "Do mercury amalgam fillings cause Alzheimer's Disease?" I then reply "You've just asked me that", to which the patient says "Who are you?"

If you are worried about

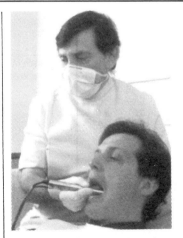

mercury amalgam fillings, do not watch *Panorama*.
© A. Dentist

"How come when he does that it's flirting, but when I do it it's harassment?"

BACKENDERS

↑ He's good looking, I **Grant** you, but **Hugh** will he choose to take home? Will it be a **Hurley** night with **Liz** or a night of **Cindy** with Ms **Crawford**?! **Hugh** knows? *(You've done that, Ed.)*

↑ Who's the Woman in **Black**!! It must be Lady **Conrad**, also known as **Barbara**! And who's her **A-miel** ticket tonight!? Step forward the millionaire Spectator columnist! Talk about **Taki**!

↑ Steady **Eddie**!! Who are you admiring so **Ardent**-ly?! Rear-ly, sir!?! Euro-in big trouble if **Neil** finds out you're dancing with his EC MP Missis!? He'll **Kinnock** your block off!!

Nunn of that in public, thank you very much!! Actress **Imogen** can't keep her hands off director hubby **Trevor**!? That's the ticket, **Stubbs**!! *(This is pathetic, Ed.)* ⇩

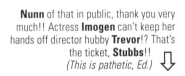

↑ Who says a **Rolling Stone** gathers no **Moss**?!! In this case, Kate certainly fits the **Bill**! The question is **Why-man**?

⇐ It's non-**Stoppard** for a busy playwright!? He shouldn't be **Tom**-fooling around with that **Lady** though!! It's a no-**Windsor** situation with her! It must be **Helen** being Royal.